Battleground

In the Footsteps of the Red Baron

With the continued expansion of the Battleground series a **Battleground Series Club** has been formed to benefit the reader. The purpose of the Club is to keep members informed of new titles and to offer many other reader-benefits. Membership is free and by registering an interest you can help us predict print runs and thus assist us in maintaining the quality and prices at their present levels.

Please call the office 01226 734555, or send your name and address along with a request for more information to:

Battleground Series Club Pen & Sword Books Ltd,
47 Church Street, Barnsley, South Yorkshire S70 2AS

Battleground Europe

In the Footsteps of the Red Baron

To Barry

Mike O'Connor
and
Norman Franks

Best wishes,

Series editor
Nigel Cave

Pen & Sword
MILITARY

This book is dedicated to Jim Davies whose name should, as a result of the enormous effort and time he has spent on the project, be on the cover credited as a co-author.

First published in Great Britain 2004, by
PEN & SWORD MILITARY
an imprint of
Pen & Sword Books Limited
47 Church Street, Barnsley, South Yorkshire S70 2AS

ISBN 1 84415 087 9

A CIP catalogue record for this book
is available from the British Library.

Printed and bound in Great Britain by
CPI UK

Cover Picture: Manfred von Richthofen in his Fokker Triplane
pursuing 'Wop' May's Camel down the Somme River valley.

Pen & Sword Books Ltd incorporates the imprints of
Pen & Sword Aviation, Pen & Sword Maritime, Pen & Sword Military,
Wharncliffe Local History, Pen & Sword Select,
Pen & Sword Military Classics and Leo Cooper.

For a complete list of Pen & Sword titles please contact:
PEN & SWORD BOOKS LIMITED
47 Church Street, Barnsley, South Yorkshire, S70 2AS, England.
E-mail: enquiries@pen-and-sword.co.uk
Website: www.pen-and-sword.co.uk

CONTENTS

Von Richthofen with two leaders of the German air force, Generals Hermann von der Leith Thomsen and Ernst von Heoppner.

INTRODUCTION BY SERIES EDITOR

Over the last eighty or more years the name of *Rittmeister* Manfred Albrecht *Frieherr* von Richthofen, the famed Red Baron of the German Air Service, has been in the forefront of military aviation history. His exploits above the Western Front between 1916 and 1918 have become almost a legend because of the number of his combat victories which, by the time of his death in April 1918, had reached an incredible 80. More books have been written about him than any other individual in the history of aviation and this volume is unlikely to be the last!

Each year many military historians and First World War enthusiasts of both the land war and the air war visit northern France to increase their interest and knowledge of the events of 1914-18. They have the opportunity to see for themselves the land above which the first air war was fought, where the airmen fell and, if they were fortunate enough to have received a decent burial, the cemetery where they rest. Because of the comparative ease with which people can now travel from Britain to France, either by ferry or by the Channel Tunnel, more and more interested parties are making the journey.

The places with evocative names that conjure up pictures of brutal warfare, of shattered towns and villages, trees and hedgerows, fields and byways, have long passed into folklore, but they are still there. They have been returned to their former states in most cases; fields that once saw the scars of battle, of trench systems, and lines of wooden crosses, or even airfields, have mostly been returned to agriculture. However, the history and the ghosts are still felt most keenly.

Following the success of Mike O'Connor's book on the airfields around Ypres, the Somme and Cambrai, it seemed that a similar book about where Manfred von Richthofen fought his air war between 1916 and 1918 would be timely and a welcome addition to the series.

The authors of this book, both keen air historians with many years of research and understanding between them, present the reader or traveller with where to go and what to see. The places of interest covered include the airfields where Richthofen flew from with *Jasta* 2, *Jasta* 11, and *Jagdgeschwader* I, the places he and his pilots would have lived, some of the places where victims fell, and the places he too was shot down.

There is nothing to compare with visiting the actual sites, seeing what the eye can scan, unlike photographs which merely show a one-dimensional image. Just a turn of the head to the left or right can bring into perspective a wholly new vista of understanding. Whatever the interest or the curiosity, this book will give both information and an insight into the first air war, and of some of the men who were involved with the famous Red Baron in those far off days.

Nigel Cave
Collegio Missionario A Rosmini,
Porta Latina, Rome.

Von Richthofen with Moritz.

ACKNOWLEDGEMENTS

We would first of all like to acknowledge the help of Peter Coles, the aviation editor for Pen and Sword Books for his help.

Secondly, I would like to thank Sylvia Menzies for the layout of the book.

We would also like to thank the following: Paul Baillie; Nigel Cave for his series introduction; Jacques de Ceuninck; the Commonwealth War Graves Commission; Bernard Deneckere for his invaluable information regarding Harlebeke and Ghistelles aerodromes; the German War Graves Commission; Hal Giblin; Barry Gray; the staff of the RAF Museum; Trevor Henshaw; Alex Imrie; Phil Jarrett; Wing Commander Jeff Jefford; Stuart Leslie for his great help with photographs; Bob Lynes; Walter Pieters; the staff of the Public Record Office; Claire Beric and Greville Raymond-Barker; Alex Revell; the staff of the *Service Historique de l'Armée de l'Air*; William Spencer; Jeff Taylor; Stewart K Taylor; the late Bruce Robertson; Les Rogers; Ray Sturtivant; Lawrie Woodcock; Barry Woodward.

Every effort has been made to contact the authors of the various books or articles quoted and their copyright is acknowledged.

USING THE GUIDE

There have been many guides to the various battlefields of the Western Front, some of them extremely detailed, but there have not been any concerning the flying aspect. Using old photographs, maps and contemporary accounts we visited old aerodrome sites and was amazed how little many of them had changed. You can hold up an old photograph of some of them and the scene behind today appears only to lack the aeroplanes. In fact many of the farms associated with these aerodromes have probably changed little in two or three hundred years.

For the military historian most of the First Wold War has a convenient chronological and geographical sequence in that one can relate how far a battle progressed (or not as the case may be) on a day-by-day basis. The air war unfortunately does not fit into this tidy pattern. Squadrons or flights would take off from one point, have a fight or range an artillery battery at another and casualties would be spread all over the front, on both sides and many miles behind the actual fighting. Casualties from a single air battle might be buried in different cemeteries miles apart.

This guide has attempted to link interesting events and individuals together, into some sort of logical and digestible order, despite the differences in time and geography. The choice of personalities and events is purely our idea of what is interesting. There has always been the glamour of the scout or fighter pilot and the 'aces' and in recent years there has been what we consider an unhealthy obsession with trying to discover 'who shot down whom'. This at best is a risky past-time, taking into account the confused nature of an air battle, the fallibility of human memory and sometimes the marked absence of German records. The air war was not just about aces but involved all the mundane tasks of photography, reconnaissance, artillery ranging, bombing, tank co-operation, infantry co-operation, supply dropping and all the myriad tasks that enabled the Allied armies win the war. To concentrate on just one aspect of the aerial battle does not do justice to the rest.

However in a book of this kind one cannot ignore the 'aces' theme, though we use the information of 'who got who' advisedly and would hope that we have presented a reasonably balanced picture of what the first air war was like.

This book has been written in the same format as Mike O'Connor's *Airfields and Airmen* series and, as such, the same principles apply. At the front is a map showing the main features in the book and then there are four separate tours, each with their own map.

THE TOURS

We have assumed that the majority of readers will be originating from the UK and thus have started the guide at Calais because of good access via the ferries and Channel Tunnel. The first chapter takes the visitor on a linear tour from Calais to Arras, which is a handy centre from which to begin the next two tours. The historic and attractive town of Arras has a number of good hotels and restaurants. Chapters Two and Three have been constructed as circular tours based on Arras. The last chapter takes the visitor back to Calais via a number of interesting sites.

Touring the sites and locations we suggest is a personal matter, depending on the interest of the traveller, the time available, or what one would like to achieve. We have suggested four itineraries, that can be done in one continuous journey, taking in a few night stops, or perhaps follow the four tours in quite separate visits. We have tried to make the journey as simple as possible, with reasonably detailed directions but the visitor – if going by car – would certainly benefit from a sensible navigator by his side with a good map; preferably a modern one, not one dated 1917!

UNKNOWN CASUALTIES

Many of von Richthofen's victims were either too badly burned to be identified by the Germans or their graves were subsequently lost. As such they are now remembered on the Air Force's Memorial to the Missing at Faubourg d'Amiens in Arras. Their names are listed in Appendix A, which will enable the visitor to pick them out during the visit to it. Because of the number of names the entry for Faubourg d'Amiens would be extremely large and thus just a few of the casualties have been selected for a potted biography. This in no way reflects on whether one person is less worthy of attention than another.

CEMETERIES

Every von Richthofen casualty has been covered and the location of graves is given at each burial ground. However, it is a good idea to take the cemetery register with you around the site as plot numbers and their positions can be confusing. In addition the excellent Commonwealth War Graves Commission website now has plans of the cemeteries for those visitors who want to plan ahead. Appendix B gives the casualties in each cemetery in the order that they appear in the book.

AERODROMES

Most of the aerodromes have diagrams so the visitor can orientate themselves and envisage where the hangars, sheds etc were located. Unfortunately for some, such as Pronville, it has been impossible to find any accurate information so visitors are directed to the relevant spot and left to use their imagination. There are also modern aerial shots to show present-day features and allow the visitor to see where all the main points are. At the back of the book are three appendices. Appendix C gives a listing of all von Richthofen's victories and the names of the crews, together with their fate. This is used in conjunction with the aerodrome visits to show the victories the Red Baron scored while based at each site. The list also indicates where the dead are buried, which will link up with the visits to cemeteries.

TABLE OF MAPS

PROLOGUE

Rittmeister Baron Manfred von Richthofen's life is so well documented that it needs little more than a brief resumé here. Born in May 1892 his military career began in 1909, like so many other young men of the time, as an army cadet. Upon graduation he became a cavalry officer with the 1st *Uhlan* Regiment and in 1914 served on the Russian Front. Later on the Western Front (France) he saw further war service but as the war became one of trench warfare rather than sweeping cavalry actions, he like many others, turned to the new dimension of aviation.

First as an observer and later a pilot, he saw duty back on the Russian Front and then once again in France. In France he was with a two-seater *abteilung* which came under the sobriquet of the Mail Carrier Pigeon Unit – (*BAO, Brieftauben-Abteilung, Ostende*), based at Ostend on the Belgian coast. This in fact was a cover name for a long distance bombing *staffel*. The unit's official designation was *Feld-fleiger Abteilung* Nr.69, or *FFA69*. This formation initially operated with Albatros BII aeroplanes and later the Albatros CI two-seater machines. *BAO's* base at Ostend was the airfield at Ghistelles.

It was not long before von Richthofen had the desire to become the

11

pilot of an aeroplane rather than just an observer – passenger – in the back seat. At first he merely asked his pilot to let him take the controls and show him how one flew; eventually he was able to keep the machine in the air satisfactorily. It was then only a short step to requesting formal pilot training, which was approved and he was off to Doberitz, just to the east of Berlin.

Once a pilot he was assigned to another bombing unit, *Kasta* 8 (*Kampfstaffel*) of *Kampfgeschwader* Nr.2 (*KG*2), flying on the French Verdun sector. This unit was then sent to Russia and it was here that he met the man than helped change his life, Oswald Boelcke. Boelcke, along with Max Immelmann and other pilots who flew the Fokker *Eindecker* fighters in 1915-16, were the first air heroes, noted for their prowess as fighter pilots using the Fokker monoplanes upon which had been fitted a machine-gun with a mechanism to allow it to fire through the whirling blades of the aeroplane's propeller. Boelcke had at his neck the blue and gold enamel *Pour le Mérite*, Germany's highest award for bravery, which in many ways became almost a magnet for other up-and-coming German fighter aces to achieve, not the least among them being the 24-year old von Richthofen.

As the 1916 Battle of the Somme rumbled on endlessly, like so many other battles and offensives of the Great War, new fighting *staffeln* were formed, one of which was given to Boelcke to command. Being such a famous air fighter, and one who had helped formulate how fighting *staffeln* should be formed and used, he was allowed to pick several pilots to man this new unit of his – *Jasta* 2 – which began operations in September 1916. Boelcke himself was killed in an air collision towards the end of October, having achieved an amazing 40 combat successes, but von Richthofen had already begun his fighting career and had achieved a number of air combat victories too by early 1917. With a personal score of 16 kills he also received the *Pour le Mérite* on 12 January and then two days later was given command of his own *staffel* – *Jasta* 11.

He continued to command this unit till 25 June 1917, at which time he was made commander of the first *Jagdgeschwader* – Nr.I – consisting of four *Jastas* (4, 6, 10 and 11), having claimed over 50 victories. From this date until his death on 21 April 1918, his victory score had risen to twice that of his mentor Boelcke, an amazing 80. This made him the highest scoring ace of any nation in the Great War.

In the Footsteps of the Red Baron

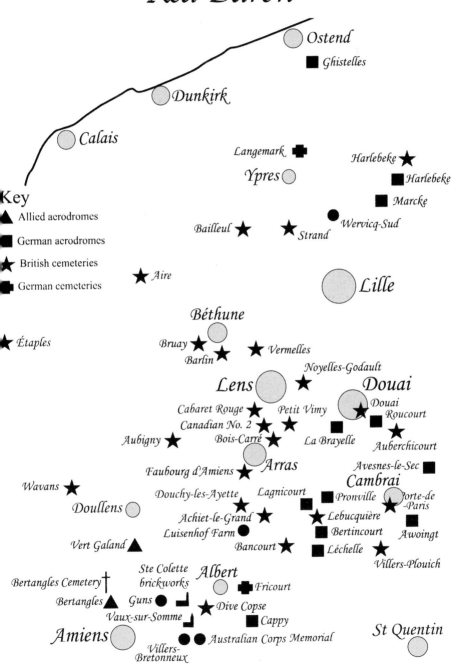

The Early Days

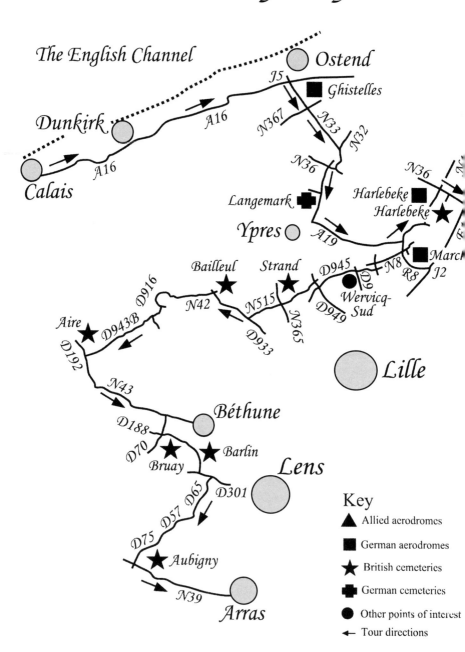

Chapter One

EARLY DAYS

The first chapter of this volume takes the visitor from the Channel Coast down to the Lens area. It encompasses von Richthofen's earliest flying experiences as an observer, and also the period towards the end of his career when he was shot down himself.

Ghistelles German Aerodrome – Von Richthofen and the *BAO*
Langemark German Cemetery – Werner Voss
Harlebeke New British Cemetery – Williams and Kember
Harlebeke German Aerodrome – *Jasta* 11
Marcke German Aerodrome – *Jagdgeschwader* Nr. 1
Wervicq-Sud – Von Richthofen shot down 6 July 1917
Strand Military Cemetery – J E Power Clutterbuck 52 Squadron
Bailleul Communal Cemetery Extension – D C Cunnell
Aire Communal Cemetery – J Hay 40 Squadron
Bruay Communal Cemetery Extension – 16 Squadron
Barlin Communal Cemetery Extension – 16 Squadron
Aubigny Communal Cemetery Extension – W J Lidsey

From Calais drive east on the A16 and exit at junction 5 then turn right on the N33 to Gistel. Turn left on the N367 to Jabbeke and follow the one-way system. Turn left at the brown Toerisme, Sport Complex, T'Ghistelhof sign, then left again on the same sign. Go right to Tennis T'Ghistelhof Park. The area ahead of you is the German aerodrome at Ghistelles.

Ghistelles German Aerodrome

Having tired of the inactivity of a cavalry regiment on the eastern front, in the winter of 1914-15 von Richthofen requested a transfer to the Air Service, his request being eventually granted in May 1915.

After training as an observer in Cologne he was posted back to the eastern front with *Feldflieger-Abteilung* 69 (*FFA*69), part of the *BAO*.

In late 1914 the Germans established a long-range bombing unit for attacking England from Calais. To mask the true intention of the unit it was given the code name of *Brieftauben-Abteilung, Ostende – BAO*

15

Ghistelles Aerodrome

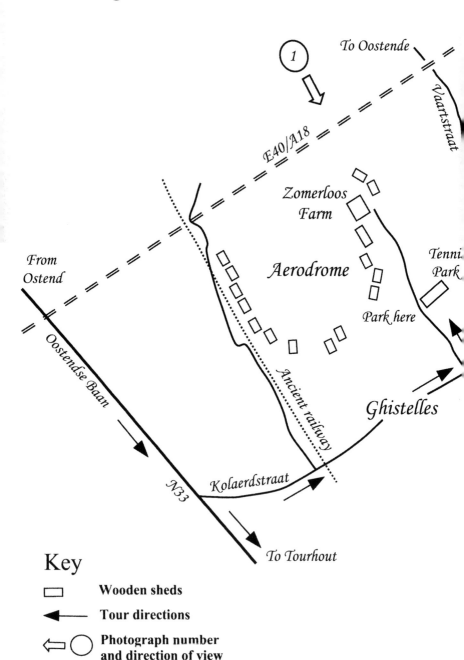

To Oostende

Vaartstraat

1

E40/A18

Zomerloos
Farm

Aerodrome

Tenni
Park

From
Ostend

Park here

Oostendse Baan

Ancient railway

Ghistelles

N33

Kolaerdstraat

To Tourhout

Key

☐   **Wooden sheds**

◄──   **Tour directions**

⇐ ◯   **Photograph number
and direction of view**

GHISTELLES

Park here

TENNIS PARK

AERODROME

FARM

Photograph No. 1: Ghistelles looking south-east in 2004.

or the Carrier Pigeon Section, Ostende. *BAO* operated Albatros B.11 two-seaters but quickly exchanged these for AEG G.II and two-seat Albatros C-types. The unit was very mobile for it had its own train so that it could be deployed rapidly to wherever support bombing-sorties were needed. When the German army failed to capture Calais the *BAO* was established near Ostend at Ghistelles aerodrome. This was too far from the UK to mount bombing operations so they were employed against targets in France. In the spring of 1915 the *BAO* was sent to the Eastern Front and two sections were detached for use in this larger campaign. They were designated *Feldflieger-Abteilung* 66 and 69 and von Richthofen joined *Feldfl-Abt* 69 in the early summer of 1915.

Having been active in Poland and Galicia against the Russians, later in the summer of 1915 the *BAO* moved back to Ghistelles. Von Richthofen's pilot was Georg Zeumer and it was he who was persuaded by the Baron to show him how to fly while out on sorties during August and September. They were flying five or six hours a day bombing and patrolling. On one occasion they had a combat with a British machine. The outcome was inconclusive and when the pair returned to Ghistelles there was a slight disagreement as to why they had not brought the enemy machine down.

Later, after the *BAO* moved south to Vouzières on the French Champagne Front, von Richthofen managed more unofficial flying instruction and by that autumn, he was fairly well advanced.

Not surprisingly, it was not long before von Richthofen was applying for formal pilot training and he left for Germany towards the end of the year.

Return to the N33 and continue south and then proceed on the N32 towards Roeselaere, then right on the R32-N32 to Menen. Turn right on the N36 signposted to Diksmuide, then turn left on the N313 to Ieper. In Poelkapelle at the Guynemer memorial go right to Langemark. In the village turn right at the lights and the cemetery will appear on the left.

Langemark German Cemetery

The cemetery itself is a huge place containing 44,000 fallen, of whom almost 25,000 are in one massed grave – the *Kameradengräb* – near to the entrance. It is in fact the only German cemetery physically situated within the Ypres salient (see also *Airfields & Airmen – Ypres* page 135).

Although this is a book devoted to von Richthofen, it would seem inappropriate to visit the area without paying tribute to another of the highest scoring German fighter aces of the First World War, Werner Voss.

Werner Voss

We are close to the place where Werner Voss was shot down. He was one of von Richthofen's former comrades while both were with *Jasta* 2. Voss was at one stage the Baron's nearest rival in terms of victories. When Voss had 48, von Richthofen was just thirteen ahead at 61.

Voss was shot down and killed in what many have recorded as one of the classic air battles of the First World War. On 23 September 1917, now with *Jasta* 10, Voss was ready to go home on leave – indeed his two brothers had arrived at the airfield at Marcke to accompany him home.

Towards the end of April 1917, von Richthofen had claimed four victories on his last day at the front prior to home leave, thereby reaching a score of 52. It may have been that Voss also wanted to go home on this leave period with a score of 50, and there is every reason to think a man of his ability could bag two more on a final flight, provided the Royal Flying Corps co-operated!

He was flying the new Fokker Triplane, and during the month he had already achieved ten victories, the last one earlier this very day. Over the same period of September 1917, von Richthofen had achieved just two kills. Admittedly the Baron had been on leave since the 6th and would not return to the Front till the final days of October, but Voss's

Manfred von Richthofen (right) talking to his rival, Werner Voss in front of an Albatros Scout. Voss scored the majority of his victories in an Albatros but was killed in action flying the new Fokker Triplane.

score was increasing. One has to wonder if, because of von Richthofen's absence from the Front, Voss was given leave so that he could not actually overtake the Baron's score while the latter was unable to score himself.

Heading out alone in the late afternoon, Voss was joined briefly by another pilot flying an Albatros Scout and over the next hour flew in action against SE5s of 60 Squadron, damaging two of them, and then virtually out-fought a patrol of half-a-dozen SE5s from 56 Squadron, achieving hits on most of them. Voss made no attempt to break off the action and seemed to relish the fight, but eventually his luck ran out. Either his fuel line or engine were hit by a burst from Lieutenant A P F Rhys Davids, and as he glided down the British pilot got behind and finished him off.

Voss, either dead or seriously wounded, crashed at Plum Farm, just north-west of Frezenberg. The location is just north-east of Ypres, along the N332. He fell inside Allied lines and was buried by the wreckage of his triplane, which the British gave the 'captured aircraft' serial G.72, although little of the machine was salvageable. It was the first triplane to fall into Allied hands, but being so near the front line it was over a month before any detailed inspection of the wreckage could be made, by which time the elements had added their toll to the damage.

For many years it was thought that Voss's grave had been lost in later fighting, but German War Graves' records show that it was later recovered and placed in the *Kameradengräb* at Langemark. His name is inscribed on panel No.63.

Return to the lights in Langemark and proceed ahead to Zonnebeke. By the Canadian memorial turn right on the N313 to Ieper. Then at the A19 turn left to Kortrijk. At the R8 turn left clockwise around Kortrijk. At junction 5 go left on the N43 to Harelbeke. Continue ahead and at traffic lights turn right and follow the green CWGC sign to the cemetery on the left.

Harlebeke New British Cemetery

Harlebeke New British Cemetery is a concentration cemetery, no graves existing here until after the end of the war. Harlebeke village was taken on the night of 19-20 October 1918 by the 9th (Scottish) Division, and the cemetery was begun after the Armistice when bodies were brought in from graves on the surrounding battlefields. Later, in 1924-25, further burials took place as bodies were transferred from German cemeteries and plots in Belgium.

More casualties were buried here during the Second World War, dating from the defence of Belgium during the retreat to Dunkirk. The cemetery now contains 1,116 First World War burials here, of which 181 are unidentified.

Of the 87 airmen represented within this total, no fewer than 25 come from No.57 Squadron RFC/RAF, lost while operating from Boisdinghem and Ste Marie-Cappel.

Two of von Richthofen's victims are buried here. The first is Second Lieutenant W H T Williams of 29 Squadron, shot down on 16 August 1917 (victory number 58), the second is Second Lieutenant W Kember of 6 Squadron, shot down on 1 September 1917 (victory number 60). Williams'grave is about half way down on the left-hand side. There are three rows at right angles to the rest of the cemetery and his grave is at the end of the back row.

William Harold Trant Williams (III C1)

On 16 August 1917, 29 Squadron's Nieuport Scouts were engaged in ground strafing German trenches around Zonnebeke and Polygon Wood, just east of Ypres. They were spotted by *Jasta* 11, and von Richthofen led the attack, chasing the Nieuports west.

It was a long chase but Richthofen's fire at last stopped the British pilot's engine. Williams's aircraft went into a spin, only recovering just above the ground. But the red Albatros was still after him and one final burst sent the Scout into the ground south-west of Houthulst Forest.

German soldiers extracted nineteen year old Williams from the wreckage and transferred him to hospital but his injuries were too severe and he died six days later.

Second Lieutenant W H T Williams of 29 Squadron.

Before he joined up, William Williams seems to have spent all his formative life in Liverpool. Born in 1898, the son of a doctor, he lived in the city at 5 Dingle Hill. After education at Liverpool College, he

Nieuport Scouts of 29 Squadron at Le Hameau in May 1917.

decided to follow his father's profession, and having passed the Northern Universities Matriculation Examination commenced an MB course at Liverpool University. Although he had successfully passed his first year examinations and already begun his second year, in 1916 he made the decision to enlist. Having already been a member of the University OTC, he was sent for training to the Inns of Court OTC on 23 October. He was next directed to the RFC Cadet School, and he was gazetted second lieutenant on 19 April 1917. Flying training followed, and he was awarded his wings in the early summer of 1917. After an initial posting to 28 Squadron in England he was sent first to No.2 Aircraft Depot in France before arriving at 29 Squadron with the grand total of 46 flying hours. He had hardly been with the squadron for any length of time before coming into deadly contact with the Red Baron.

Walter Kember (XII A8)

The next grave is situated approximately halfway down the cemetery on the right-hand side and is in the middle of the front row of plot XII.

There were many instances of aircrew being killed within a few days of arrival at their first squadron, and this occurred in Kember's case, although his end appears an exceptionally unfair and sad one.

Von Richthofen was flying a Fokker Triplane for the first time and attacked the RE8 near Zonnebeke. At the time, the only triplanes known to Kember and his pilot, Lieutenant John B C Madge, were Allied Sopwith Triplanes operated by the Royal Naval Air Service. Kember's last thoughts may have been, why is this naval flyer coming at us, is he having a bit of fun, or does he think we are a German machine? Might it even be a German pilot in a captured Sopwith?

Second Lieutenant Walter Kember, 6 Squadron, killed in action 1 September 1917 – Richthofen's first victim flying in a Triplane.

We will never know, but in his report von Richthofen said that the observer made no move to fire back at him and was standing upright in his rear cockpit. It was quickly over as Kember was hit by the Baron's fire, while Madge was wounded in the back.

Walter Kember was the son of a dentist (also named Walter) from 'Sarina', 5 Dover Road, Birkdale, near Southport, Lancashire. Like William Williams he had also attended Liverpool University, and also planned to follow his father's profession, studying for a Licentiate in Dental Surgery when war broke out.

An RE8 of 34 Squadron. This type of machine was a great improvement on the BE2. The observer was behind the pilot and had a good field of fire. A well organised crew were more than a match for a German Albatros.

He immediately volunteered, and left his studies to join his local territorial battalion as a private in the 7/King's Liverpool Regiment. He went to France with his unit on 8 March 1915, so had only been abroad for a few days when he went over the top on 15 May, the first day of the Battle of Festubert. He was wounded during the fighting, suffering flesh wounds in the legs. After recovering from his injuries in a London hospital he was selected for officer training, and was then commissioned as second lieutenant in the 7/Lancashire Fusiliers. He transferred to the RFC in July 1917. Following training as an observer he was sent to 6 Squadron, based at Abeele, flying RE8s. Again like Williams, he had only been with his squadron for a few days when he was killed.

John Madge survived his wounds and the subsequent crash and was taken prisoner. He spent much of his captivity in German hospitals until he was finally repatriated on 17 December 1918. Madge's hospitalisation continued for some months before he was finally able to return to the medical studies he had begun at Edinburgh University in 1912. It would be some twelve years later that he would finally qualify as a Doctor of Medicine (MB ChB Univ Edin). His medical career took him all over the country, practising in East Ealing, London, then Shipton-Thorpe, York, and Shirebrook, Nottingham before he retired to the tiny village of Newton by Toft, Lincolnshire. It was there that he died in 1957 at the age of 65.

Return to the traffic lights and turn left to Centrum. At the next set of lights turn right onto the N36. At the roundabout proceed towards Bavikhove E17. Take the first left after the roundabout into a housing estate. Continue straight ahead over a pavé chicane and stop at the next area of pavé, where the road bends to the right. Ahead can be seen a farm. The area this side of the farm was the German aerodrome at Harlebeke.

Harlebeke German Aerodrome

Harlebeke airfield was the home of *Jasta* 11 before it moved to Courtrai/Marckebeke. (The flying field is actually a couple of kilometres due north, near Bavikhove, close to the River Lys and just before it is joined by the canal from Roeselare.)

Von Richthofen was here from 10 June to 1 July 1917 during which time he claimed four British aircraft – victories 53 to 56 – two RE8s, a Spad and a DH4. The crew of victory number 53, Lieutenants R W Ellis and H C Barlow of 9 Squadron have no known grave and are commemorated at Arras. Claim No.54 was Lieutenant R W Farquhar (see page 79). Number 55 was the crew of a 57 Squadron DH4, Captain N G McNaughton and Lieutenant A H Mearns, who also have no known grave and are commemorated at Arras. The final victory while based at Harlebeke was an RE8 crew from 53 Squadron. The name of the pilot, Lieutenant L S Bowman, is inscribed on the Arras memorial but his observer Second Lieutenant J E Power Clutterbuck is buried in Strand Military Cemetery (see page 33)

The commander of the German Air Service, General Ernst von Hoeppner, knew they were encountering ever larger formations of Allied machines and he realised that in order to be effective he would have to combine several *jastas*. Initially *Jastas* 6, 7, 11 and 26 were envisaged for this new unit which was termed a *jagdgeschwader*. Von Richthofen with his growing reputation was the obvious candidate to

Photograph No. 2: Harlebeke in 2004 looking east.

Harlebeke Aerodrome

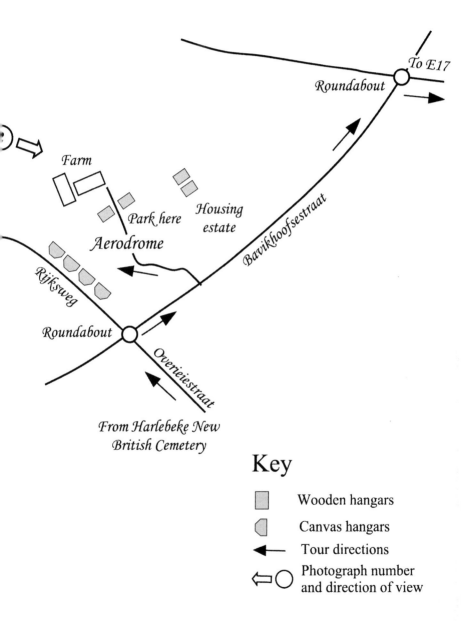

Roundabout

To E17

Farm

Park here

Aerodrome

Housing estate

Bavikhoofsestraat

Rijksweg

Roundabout

Overieiestraat

From Harlebeke New British Cemetery

Key

Wooden hangars

Canvas hangars

Tour directions

Photograph number and direction of view

lead it. To enhance his chance of success two units were replaced: *Jastas* 7 and 26 were exchanged with 4 and 10.

On the afternoon of 25 June 1917 Manfred von Richthofen was formally appointed commander of *Jagdgeschwader* I. A new aerodrome at Marcke, near Courtrai was prepared for the unit and the château of Castle de Béthune was commandeered as accommodation (see the next entry in this tour).

Return to main road and turn left. At the first roundabout go right towards the E17. Continue ahead following E17 signs. At the E17 turn left to Kortrijk. At junction 2 leave E17 on the R8 Kortrijk West. Follow Andere Richtinger then R8 Kortrijk West. Leave at junction 11 on the N8 to Wevelgem. At the top of the sliproad turn right for Kortrijk and at the first traffic lights turn for Marke. Continue ahead over the metal bridge and Marke aerodrome is on the left.

Marcke and Marckebeke German Aerodromes

JG I was based near Courtrai from 1 July to 22 November 1917 and von Richthofen claimed victories 57 to 61 while stationed here. F G B Pascoe and H A Whatley of 53 Squadron have no known grave and their names are inscribed on the Arras memorial, as is C P Williams of 19 Squadron. Walter Kember killed on 1 September figures on page 22 while W H T Williams of 29 Squadron features on page 21.

There are in fact two airfields here in very close proximity. The one you have now arrived by is Marcke, which lies south of the railway line

Photograph No. 3: Marcke looking south in 2001.

Marckebeke and 'Marcke' Aerodromes

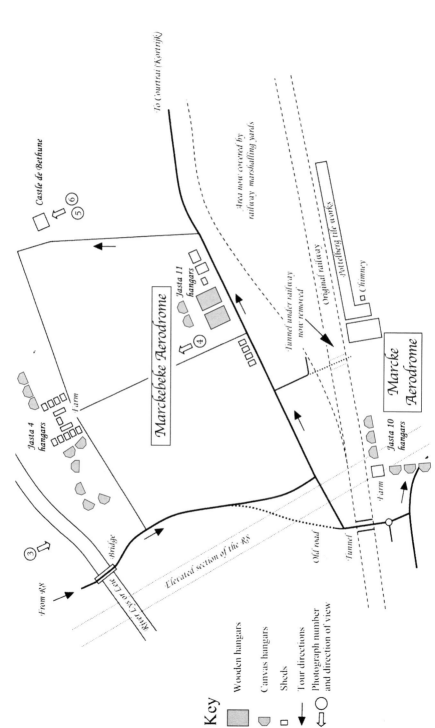

Castle de Bethune

Jasta 11 hangars

Marckebeke Aerodrome

Jasta 4 hangars

Farm

Marcke Aerodrome

Jasta 10 hangars

Farm

To Courtrai (Kortrijk)

Area now covered by railway marshalling yards

Tunnel under railway now removed

Original railway

Potteberg tile works

Chimney

River Lys or Leie

Bridge

From R8

Elevated section of the R8

Old road

Tunnel

Key

Wooden hangars

Canvas hangars

Sheds

Tour directions

Photograph number and direction of view

Photograph No. 4: The 'famous' picture of Richthofen introducing General Ludendorf to his pilots, with the Baron's red Albatros in the background. The road leads to *Jasta* 4's farmhouse area.

and has now virtually disappeared under a flyover and a factory area.

Immediately to the east of the old airfield area is the Pottelberg Tile Works. The original rail line ran past this building, but today the line turns slightly north-east before it reaches the Works and then runs to a marshalling yard. The area between the road and the works was where *Jasta* 10 of *JG* I was based, mostly under the command of Werner Voss, until he was killed flying from here on 23 September 1917 (see page 18).

Another item of interest is that *Jasta* 11's Kurt Wolff crash-landed on the railway line after being wounded in the hand during a fight with Sopwith Triplanes of 1 Naval Squadron on 11 July 1917. He was trying to reach Marckebeke immediately to the north, but failed, ending up on the rail tracks. His undercarriage was ripped off in the process and he turned over, the fuselage of his Albatros Scout coming to rest on a fence.

There is today not a great deal to see at this airfield location, but driving north through the rail archway, the immediate right turn takes you along the road which borders the south-side of the site of the main airfield, used by *Jasta* 11 and *Jasta* 4. This is Marckebeke.

In contrast to Marcke, little has changed since it was an airfield. Half way along the road is a narrow track heading roughly north, which leads

28

Photograph No. 5: *Jasta* **11 pilots on the rear steps of the château with Wolff nursing his injured left hand after being wounded on 11 July 1917.**

Photograph No. 6: The same château steps taken eighty-two years later.

to the farm with a farmhouse and buildings. It was here that *Jasta* 4 was based with its hangars and tents. Immediately to the east of the farm road, and bordering the main Courtrai road, was where *Jasta* 11 had its hangars and workshops.

One of the famous photographs of *JG* I was taken at this spot during an inspection visit by General Erich von Ludendorff. The photograph of von Richthofen introducing his *Jasta* 11 pilots to the General was taken by a cameraman on top of one of the workshop buildings. In the picture is von Richthofen's red Albatros DV, the pilot's ladder leaning up against the fuselage by the cockpit. In front of this machine can be seen the farm road leading to *Jasta* 4.

The fourth *staffel* in the *Jagdgeschwader*, *Jasta* 6, was at this time based at Bisseghem just north of the Lys. Today Bisseghem has virtually disappeared. Just to the west the airfield at Wevelgem has been extended over the years, taking over the area once occupied by the Bisseghem airfield. There is a nice little air museum run by the Flying Club (along with the 'Biggles' Restaurant on *Lufthaven Str.*). This is not generally open to the public, but enquiries before your visit might persuade the Club to let you have a look around.

JG I's officers took over the nearby château, the Castle de Béthune, which is situated just to the east of the main airfield, surrounded by trees, but within a couple of minutes walk to both *Jasta* 11 and *Jasta* 4's hangars. By car it would have taken someone from the château only a few minutes to drive round to Marcke and Voss's *Jasta* 10 and only a little longer to reach *Jasta* 6.

The Castle was built in 1802 and the Béthune family have lived there for several generations. (It remains private property, and visitors are reminded to seek permission if they wish to see the château) They were forced to move into a few upstairs rooms while *JG* I's officers took over the rest of the building.

Several photographs have been taken of von Richthofen and his pilots on the steps of both the front entrance door and the rear door, the latter leading out to a garden and small pond.

It was from Marckebeke that von Richthofen flew from on the day (6 July 1917) he was wounded, just a few days after starting operations from here (see page 31). There are photographs of him on the steps of the building while his head was still swathed in bandages following his stay in St Nicholas's Hospital, and it was here that he returned to active flying in August 1917.

By then he was an 'older and wiser' man, having realised perhaps that he was just as vulnerable as anyone to sudden death or injury. Some say he was never the same again.

Return to the N8 and turn left, continuing ahead until the N32. Go left on the N32 then right on the N366 Centrum. Follow the one-way system and turn left for Halluin then right for Bousbecque. Follow signs for Bousbecque and Wervicq-Sud. Turn left on the D9 to Linselles. At the roundabout go right and at the cross roads follow the German cemetery signs. Continue ahead and the cemetery is on the left.

Wervicq-Sud

The hill behind the cemetery is La Montagne and von Richthofen landed somewhere in the large open area in front of you.

Wervicq-Sud is where von Richthofen was shot down on 6 July 1917 – not the more obvious town of Wervicq. He and his pilots were attacking a formation of FE2b 'pushers' of 20 Squadron, and von Richthofen appears to have made the mistake of pursuing one a little too long without taking sufficient evasive action. This allowed the observer in one of the FEs, Lieutenant A E Woodbridge (it has always been assumed), to get in a damaging burst at the Red Baron. Von Richthofen was hit across the top of his skull. A fraction of an inch either way would have missed him completely or ended his life.

For a moment von Richthofen was completely paralysed. His hands dropped to his side, his legs slipped off the rudder bar and as his optic nerve had been numbed, he lost all

Von Richthofen with his bandaged head wound.

Von Richthofen's forced landing, on 6 July 1917, at Wervicq-Sud.

power of sight. It must have been quite a moment, knowing that he was in the air, blind and paralysed. He was fortunate in that his Albatros DV did not go into a spin, leaving him little time to recover, even if he regained some feeling in his limbs. As it happened, he did regain some mobility and his sight returned at about a height of 800 metres.

He immediately switched off his engine, spotted an open space below where he could land, and within moments rolled to a stop in a grassy meadow close to a road, just to the south of Wervicq-Sud. Two of his pilots had followed him down and circled.

Von Richthofen climbed out, blood streaming form his head wound, and collapsed. An officer and a corporal at La Montagne, a mile to the south, ran to the spot and found the wounded airman lying still by his machine. They administered first-aid, then the corporal ran back to call for an ambulance. Not long afterwards the Baron was taken to St Nicholas's Hospital (*Feldlazarett* Nr.76) in the town of Courtrai. There is still a hospital on the site although the original was torn down in the 1960s to make room for a larger building.

The officer who tended him by the Albatros was *Leutnant* Hans Schröder, who recounted the episode in his book *An Airman Remembers* (John Hamilton, 1936). Schröder had been a soldier and an airman before becoming Air Defence Officer for the Wytschaete Army Group in late June 1917. He was based at the observation post on the top of La Montagne, an area of high ground (just 55 metres above sea level, so not a large hill) located south of Wervicq-Sud, where his job was to observe air activity to the west.

From here, along with the officer he was replacing, he had seen von Richthofen shoot down his 56th victory on 25 June – J E Power Clutterbuck (see page 24). Schröder had watched fascinated through a telescope. Moments later the red Albatros itself flew directly over the observation post, its pilot waving down at the German observers, needing them to confirm his latest victory. In his book Schröder says they also watched another British aircraft shot down over Ypres, this time by *Jasta* 11's Karl Allmenröder.

There are a number of photographs of Richthofen's Albatros DV after the forced landing, which appears to have an all-red tail section and wings, nose/spinner, struts and wheel covers. In one of them two tall factory chimneys can be seen, which must be in Wervicq-Sud. Therefore the field in which he force-landed has to be just south of the town, and just west of the La Montagne high-ground – in other words, just west of the D9.

Schröder had again watched the fight with the FEs through his telescope, and watched too as the Albatros (although he called it a Fokker in his book) came towards him after a headlong dive, flattened out and landed about one kilometre away. Seeing the pilot climb out, then collapse, he and his corporal immediately ran down the slope of the hill and went to the pilot's aid.

Just three days earlier, on 3 July, Schröder had watched Albert Dossenbach jump from his burning Albatros during a fight with British aircraft above Frezenberg, just east of Ypres, from his La Montagne location. Dossenbach was commanding *Jasta* 10 in Richthofen's *JG* I.

Return to the cross roads and turn left to the D945 and left to Comines. After crossing the river Deule go right on the D949 to a T junction. Turn left on the N515 to Ploegsteert. At the roundabout turn right on the N365 to Ieper. The cemetery is on the right.

Strand Military Cemetery

The cemetery acquired its name from a trench which led into Ploegsteert Wood. A couple of burials were made here in October 1914, when there was an advanced dressing station nearby. It was then not used until April 1917, when further burials were made.

It was in German hands for a few months in 1918, but was only used again after the end of the fighting when bodies were brought in from nearby smaller cemeteries and the battlefields, mostly between Wytschaete and Armentières. It now contains 1,143 Commonwealth servicemen, of whom 354 are unidentified. There are also eight Second World War burials, dating from May 1940 during the retreat to Dunkirk.

The cemetery contains the graves of eight airmen and of these one is a victim of the Red Baron. He is buried in the long plot that forms the right side of the centre aisle and is half way along it. The grave is towards the end of the row.

James Edward Power Clutterbuck (IX I 7)
Power Clutterbuck was the observer in a 53 Squadron RE8 piloted by Lieutenant Lesley Spencer Bowman, which was shot down on 25 June 1917 – just three weeks after Power Clutterbuck had joined the squadron – becoming von Richthofen's 56th victory. They were shot down over the trenches near Le Bizet, the wings breaking off the RE8 as it fell, landing in No Man's Land between the two front lines.

The only son of the late Surgeon Major E R Power Clutterbuck

AMS, James came from Dursley, Gloucestershire, and was born on 21 July 1894. He had joined up as a private soldier in October 1914 before being gazetted as a second lieutenant in the Royal Field Artillery on 29 January 1915.

He had seen service in Gallipoli and on the Western Front, being wounded in both theatres of war, before successfully transferring to the Royal Flying Corps. He had been with 53 Squadron for just three weeks before he was shot down and killed.

Bowman, also the son of a doctor, and also an only son, came from Ulverston, Lancashire, and was born on 21 June 1897. Educated at Seascale Preparatory School and Clifton College, he joined up as soon as he was old enough, and was gazetted a second lieutenant in the 4th(Territorial) Battalion Kings Own Royal Lancaster Regiment on 23 December 1914.

Arriving at the Front a year later in December 1915, he served in the Picardy and Arras areas, being slightly wounded on 7 May 1916 when a bullet, which had already passed through another man standing alongside, struck him.

He transferred to the RFC in July 1916 and was given his wings on 24 September 1916. He returned to France on 23 December, exactly two years to the day since he had been first gazetted, but this time as a pilot in the Royal Flying Corps.

Promoted to lieutenant on 4 January 1917, he was slightly wounded on 6 June but was

Lieutenant L S Bowman, 53 Squadron, killed in action on 25 June 1917.

passed fit to resume his duties on 20 June and was able to celebrate his birthday in the Mess the following day. Just four days later he was dead. He has no known grave, and is commemorated on the Air Services Memorial to the Missing at Arras (see page 83), although his observer's body was recovered by British troops and given a decent burial.

Return to the roundabout and go right to Neuve-Église. At an unsignposted T-junction, turn left. In Nieppe turn right at a roundabout on the D933 to Bailleul. In Bailleul turn right at the traffic lights signposted to Loker and Ieper. Take the first right at the CWGC green sign and the cemetery is on the right.

Bailleul Communal Cemetery Extension

Apart from a short period between April and August 1918, Bailleul was in Allied hands for the rest of the war. It was an important railway and hospital centre, with the 2nd, 3rd, 8th, 11th, 53rd, 1st Canadian and 1st Australian Casualty Clearing Stations being based here for considerable periods.

The earliest burials were made in the communal cemetery until the space was filled which occurred in April 1915. After this the extension was opened to the east of the original cemetery, and burials continued here (apart from the months of German occupation) for the rest of the war and beyond, when casualties were brought in from the neighbouring battlefields.

There are 610 burials in the Communal section and 4,403 in the extension. In addition there are seventeen Second World War burials, and 154 German burials from both wars.

As one would expect from a cemetery adjacent to the site of three important airfields (see *Airfields & Airmen: Ypres* page 54) there is a large RFC/RAF representation with 77 graves. Of these twelve are from 53 Squadron based literally across the road from the cemetery at the Town Ground aerodrome, another twelve are from 1 Squadron based a mile away at The Asylum aerodrome, and fourteen are from 20 Squadron based some twelve kilometres to the west at Ste. Marie-Cappel.

Perhaps 20 Squadron's most famous pilot is Tom Mottershead VC DCM, the only RFC non-officer to earn a Victoria Cross. He died of injuries on 12 January 1917 and is buried in grave III A 126 (see *Airfields & Airmen: Ypres* page 61).

But today we have come to pay our tributes to another 20 Squadron pilot who features in the von Richthofen story. The grave of Donald Charles Cunnell is located in the far left corner of the cemetery just a short distance from the transverse aisle.

An RE8 of 25 Squadron after wiping its undercarriage off at Bailleul. On the right are the hangars of the Town Ground aerodrome. On the left is the military cemetery.

Donald Charles Cunnell (III C 263)

It was Norwich-born Captain Donald Cunnell whose observer, A E Woodbridge, was credited with downing von Richthofen on 6 July 1917, when he force landed at Wervicq-Sud (see page 31). Cunnell was seconded to the RFC from the Hampshire Regiment joining at Reading on 5 August 1916 and after attending the Central Flying School and 28 Reserve Squadron he was gazetted a flying officer on 24 November 1916. He was posted direct from 28 RS to 20 Squadron in France only five days later. On 14 May 1917 he was promoted to flight commander.

Just a few days after the Richthofen fight on 11 July Cunnell, with another man in the front cockpit of his FE2b, was killed in the air by an exploding AA shell. His observer, Lieutenant A G Bill, took over the controls and flew the FE back to base at Ste Marie-Cappel,

Lieutenant A E Woodbridg credited with wounding th Baron on 6 July 1917, whi flying with Captain D C Cunnell, 20 Squadron.

thus ensuring Cunnell was buried by his own people. He had been with the squadron for seven months and he, together with his various observers, had claimed nine victories.

Follow the one-way system back to the traffic lights and turn left on the D933 to Cassel and Hazebrouck. At the roundabout go left on the D944 to Strazeele and Hazebrouck. At the roundabout turn right on the N42 to Béthune. Follow Béthune signs across the roundabouts and continue on the D916 to Béthune then proceed right on the D943B to Steenbecque and Aire-sur-la-Lys. Pass through the town, ahead at the traffic lights and at the T junction right on the D192 to St Omer. Immediately before the roundabout turn right down a slip road and the cemetery is on the right.

Aire Communal Cemetery

Entry to the cemetery is by a small gate to the right of the keeper's house. Proceed up the hill towards the French and British flags. An unusual feature of this civil cemetery is the number of French military white crosses spread throughout it. Entering the military cemetery from the civilian burial ground continue past the Cross of Sacrifice to the Stone of Remembrance. Row H is to the right and is at right angles to the other rows. John Hay's grave (I H 7) is about half way along.

For most of the war, Aire was a busy but peaceful centre behind the lines used at various times by different Commonwealth forces as corps headquarters. The Highland Casualty Clearing Station was based here, as was the 39th Stationary Hospital from May 1917, and earlier burials date from this period.

After the second, 'Georgette', German spring offensive of 1918 the 54th Casualty Clearing Station was based here, and for a while Aire was within thirteen kilometres of the front line.

In all there are 894 Commonwealth graves from the Great War plus a few French and German graves. There are also 21 Second World War burials, mostly dating from the retreat to Dunkirk in May 1940.

There are 49 RFC/RAF graves, including twelve from No.22 Squadron, six from 42 Squadron and just two from 40 Squadron, one of whom we have come to visit – John Hay.

John Hay (I H 7)

John 'Jack' Hay was with 40 Squadron, flying FE8 'pusher' scouts, and after a fight with Richthofen on the afternoon of 23 January 1917, was seen to fall – or jump – from his burning aeroplane and plunge to the ground. It was the German's 17th victory. Eight *Jasta* 11 machines had engaged the FE8s southwest of Lens and the Baron's target had caught fire after he had fired 150 rounds into it. Canadian troops recovered Hay's shattered body which had fallen well inside British lines. His squadron must have claimed his remains as he had taken off from their base at Treizennes, only three or so kilometres from the cemetery but had crashed more than 30 kilometres away.

Australian Jack Hay, 40 Squadron, killed in action, 23 January 1917.

Jack Hay was born on 22 January 1889 at Double Bay, an affluent suburb of Sydney, New South Wales. He was the son of William and Isabella Hay, and came from a well-to-do family, his great, great uncle had been Sir John Hay, who had come to Australia from England in 1838.

Jack was educated at Shore, the Sydney Church of England Grammar School, and at the outbreak of war he was living in Warren, a lush grazing area in the Central West of New South Wales. Arriving

The FE8 was an elegant design but due to production delays was out-classed by the German Albatros when it arrived on the Western Front.

in England in early 1916 he gained his Royal Aero Club Certificate, number 3039, on 2 June and volunteered for service with the Royal Flying Corps.

Posted to 40 Squadron in France, Jack Hay was no novice and had already claimed three German aircraft shot down, the third one falling on the morning of this fateful day. It was one day past his 28th birthday.

After the war, his mother donated a bell, inscribed in her son's name, to the Carillon built in 1923 by Sydney University to commemorate the sacrifice of its students during the Great War.

Return to the roundabout and proceed south on the N43 towards Béthune. Then turn right on the D70 to Labeuvrière. At the roundabout go left on the D188 to Bruay-la-Buissière. At the top of the hill go right signposted 2AL No.3. At the roundabout follow the Cimetière Ouest and continue to the cemetery on the left.

Bruay Communal Cemetery Extension

French soldiers began this cemetery in late 1914, on land belonging to the *Compagnie des Mines de Bruay*. The area's connection with coal mining is shown by the large slag heap in the field opposite the main entrance to the civil cemetery. The extension is towards the far right corner of the main cemetery, just beyond a rather graphic memorial to various members of the local civilian population who were killed during the Second World War, and whose commemorative plaques have now been moved to the cemetery.

After the British took over this part of the line in March 1916, the 22nd Casualty Clearing Station was established in Bruay and continued to use the cemetery. Nearly half the burials here are from the Canadian Corps who occupied this sector of the front in 1917.

There are 412 graves plus a number of French and German. Of the sixteen airmen, no less than eleven are from No.16 Squadron who were based at Bruay from August 1916 to May 1917 (flying BE2s and RE8s), and include three of the Baron's victims, Quicke, Watt and Howlett. Their graves are all in row D, the fourth row from the back, facing away from you. That of Quicke is just over half way down the row, with Watt and Howlett just beyond.

There is also an RFC ace, John Lancashire Barlow of 40 Squadron, shot down by *Jasta* 12 on the same day Voss was killed, 23 September 1917. His grave is situated in the middle of the second row from the front. Flying a Nieuport Scout he claimed six German machines during June, July and August but was then killed in action.

George Macdonald Watt (D 7) and Ernest Adam Howlett (D 8)

George Watt and Ernest Howlett in their BE2g were no match for Richthofen's Albatros when he met up with them on 17 March 1917, even though they did have aircraft in the sky above offering some kind of protection.

Richthofen therefore dived below the BE and attacked from that position, more than likely in the British crew's blind spot. His fire raked the two-seater and both its wings came away, sending the crew in the shattered fuselage down into No Man's Land, where it was hit by gunfire from the German trenches. It was his 28th victory.

Twenty-seven year old George Watt, from Edinburgh, was the son of George Watt KC, the Sheriff of Inverness, Elgin and Nairn, and his wife Jessie. After education at Fettes College, he left in 1907

G. MacDonald Watt, 16 Squadron, killed in action, 17 March 1917.

to attend Edinburgh University. In 1912 he secured a position with a British timber company operating in Burma, before returning in July 1916 to fight for King and Empire.

He joined the Royal Flying Corps, and was trained at Turnhouse, near Edinburgh, and at Montrose. He gained his 'wings' on 6 January

1917 and soon afterwards, on 17 January was posted to 16 Squadron.

Ernest Howlett, from New Cross, south-east London, who was a year younger than his pilot, had lived with his widowed mother before volunteering for service with the East Kent Regiment (The Buffs) at the outbreak of the war. An outstanding soldier, he was promoted to sergeant in the trenches before returning home for transfer to the RFC, and, following training as an observer, he was posted to 16 Squadron.

Sidney Herbert Quicke (D 12)

Flight Sergeant S H Quicke of 16 Squadron, was the pilot of the crew shot down to become von Richthofen's 29th victory on 21 March 1917. He was killed in the crash but his observer, Second Lieutenant W J Lidsey, was pulled out alive though seriously injured. Lidsey died early the next morning which is why he is buried in another cemetery, Aubigny Communal Cemetery Extension (see page 45).

Sidney Quicke had been in the RFC since 1913, initially as a mechanic, and was one of the first to go to France as an air mechanic first class with 4 Squadron on 12 August 1914, qualifying him for the Mons Star. By 1916 he was a sergeant, and qualified as an observer on 31 March. Later the same year he went on to pilot training, and received his Royal Aero Club Aviator's Certificate, number 3890, on 27 November 1916, his RFC pilot's wings being awarded soon afterwards.

Flight Sergeant S H Quicke of 16 Squadron, who fell to the Baron on 21 March 1917.

Return to the D188 and go right to Bruay-la-Bussière. At a roundabout go ahead to Centre Ville. At the traffic lights go ahead on the D188 to Barlin. Continue over the roundabouts until you reach one where you go left on the D188 to Barlin Centre. Take the first left at the green CWGC sign and the cemetery is on the right.

Barlin Communal Cemetery Extension

The extension was originally begun by French troops in October 1914, and used by them until they moved south in March 1916 when this part of the Front was taken over by Commonwealth forces, the cemetery then being used by 6th Casualty Clearing Station.

In December 1917 the hospital moved back to Ruitz when the area around Barlin began to be shelled, but the extension was used again in March and April 1918 during the German offensive.

The burial ground contains 1,094 graves, plus a number of French and German. Most unusually, along the front of the cemetery to either side of the entrance is a row of graves of French miners killed in a colliery accident in 1917.

Eight graves belong to aviators, half being 16 Squadron personnel, two of whom were shot down by the Red Baron. The graves of Gerald Gosset-Bibby and Geoffrey Brichta are in the very back row of the cemetery against the wall, about three quarters of the way down the row to the right.

BE2c 4072. No. 16 Squadron employed the BE2 in its various marks from May 1915 until late summer 1917 when they were fully equipped with RE8s.

41

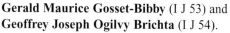

Gerald Maurice Gosset-Bibby (I J 53) and
Geoffrey Joseph Ogilvy Brichta (I J 54).

Von Richthofen shot Gosset-Bibby and Brichta down on 6 March 1917. They were his 24th victory, another BE crew, and yet another machine that lost its wings as it plummeted earthwards, giving the crew no chance of survival. Their machine came down just inside the British lines near Souchez a few minutes after 1600 hours, some two and a quarter hours after they had taken off from Bruay on an artillery observation flight over Vimy.

Gerald Gosset-Bibby was the only son of the Reverend Arthur G and Mrs A Gosset-Bibby. He was born on 9 April 1897 at Kimbolton, Huntingdonshire, where his father was headmaster at the local grammar school, although he had retired by the outbreak of war and the family were living at 11 St. Augustine Road, Bedford. After prep school at Wells House, Malvern Wells, Gerald attended Oundle School as a boarder from 1911 to 1914.

He enlisted in the RFC as soon as he was old enough and served as an NCO observer during the Battle of the Somme in 1916, before returning to England for pilot training and a commission. Gazetted a flying officer he returned to France, and joined 16 Squadron in February 1917. He was killed just one month later, still a month short of his twentieth birthday.

Geoffrey Brichta, was 32 years old. He was born in Austria of British parents, his father being a doctor practising in Vienna. After his father's death his mother Marina returned to England with her young son and they eventually settled at Eastwood House, Northwood, Middlesex. Geoffrey was musically gifted and sang in Chichester Cathedral.

He migrated to Canada in 1908, and four years later had settled in Battleford, Saskatchewan where he used his musical talents, running the North Battleford Piano Company. He was also a member of the local militia unit, the 22nd Battalion, Saskatchewan Light Horse.

Second Lieutenant G M Gossett-Bibby, 16 Squadron, killed in action with his observer, Lieutenant G J O Brichta, 6 March 1917.

Geoffrey Brichta, 16 Squadron, aged 32.

42

In November 1915 he left Canada for England with the 9th Canadian Mounted Rifles, leaving behind a wife and three young children. Having transferred to the 2nd Battalion, he arrived in France in March 1916 before moving again to the RFC where he was taken on strength as an observer in September 1916.

Brichta joined 16 Squadron on probation on 7 October 1916 and was something of a rarity, firstly because of his age, being 32 when he died, and secondly being a Canadian observer, as although there were a significant number of Canadian pilots, there were only ever a handful of Canadian observers.

Return to the roundabout and go left signposted A21-A26. At another roundabout go ahead on the D179E to Houdain. At yet another roundabout proceed ahead on the D57 E2 signposted A26 Reims. Pass under a dual carriageway and at a roundabout go left on the D301 to Lens. Leave Hersin-Coupigny and at a T junction turn left and continue on the road which becomes the D65 then the D57. Turn right on the D75 to Estrée-Cauchy. At a cross roads go ahead on the D75 to Aubigny-en-Artois. At a T junction turn right to the next roundabout and turn left following the green CWGC Aubigny Communal Cemetery Extension sign up the hill.

Aubigny Communal Cemetery Extension

This area was taken over from the French in March 1916, and burials were made here until September 1918. The 42nd Casualty Clearing Station used the extension throughout the period, with the 30th, 24th, 1st Canadian and 57th also employing the cemetery. There are now 2,771 First War and seven Second War burials here, as well as 227 French and 64 Germans.

There are 82 fliers buried here, one of the highest numbers in a single cemetery on the Western Front. Of these 24 are from 16 Squadron, based at Bruay and Camblain L'Abbe; sixteen are from 5 Squadron based at Savy, Acq and Le Hameau; and ten are from 13 Squadron, based at Savy from March 1916 to May 1917.

Having walked through the French civilian cemetery, look left at the Extension entrance and you will see two plots of graves with the headstones at right angles to the others, facing across the cemetery towards the Stone of Remembrance. Plot V is to the left, with Plot VI to its right. The grave of William Lidsey is in Plot V, and is seventh from the right hand end, backed against the hedge.

Mortally wounded on 21 March 1917, Second Lieutenant W J Lidsey died the next morning.

William John Lidsey (V A 38)

We met Lidsey earlier when we visited the grave of Sergeant Sidney Quicke, buried in Bruay Cemetery (see page 40). You will recall that Lidsey was the observer in von Richthofen's 29th victory on 21 March 1917. Although Quicke, the pilot, was already dead when pulled from the wreckage, Lidsey survived the fall of his machine for a short time.

Born in 1895, William Lidsey was the son of Councillor William I R and Mrs Emily Crozier Lidsey of 'Hardwick House', Banbury, Oxfordshire. He was educated at Magdelene College School, Brackley, and had not long embarked on his business career, training as an auctioneer and valuer, when war broke out. With many of his friends he helped to form the 1/4 (Territorial) Battalion of the Oxfordshire and Buckinghamshire Light Infantry, landing at Boulogne on 30 March 1915.

After a period in the trenches he returned home for officer training, and was gazetted second lieutenant on 2 February 1916, rejoining his old regiment in June the same year. After a further period in the trenches until November 1916 he joined the RFC as an observer.

Shot down during his second patrol of the day, William Lidsey was barely alive when pulled from the wreckage but survived long enough to reach a field hospital and so be separated from his pilot. The severity of his injuries can be judged from the rather forthright message received by his parents:-

Your son was admitted on the evening of Wednesday, 21st, mortally wounded in the head and legs and an operation was impossible, he was partly conscious when he was brought in but passed away 3 o'clock Thursday morning.

Return to the roundabout at the top of the hill and turn left. At the give way sign turn left on to the main road and then turn left on to the N39 to Arras. This completes the first itinerary.

The Central Area

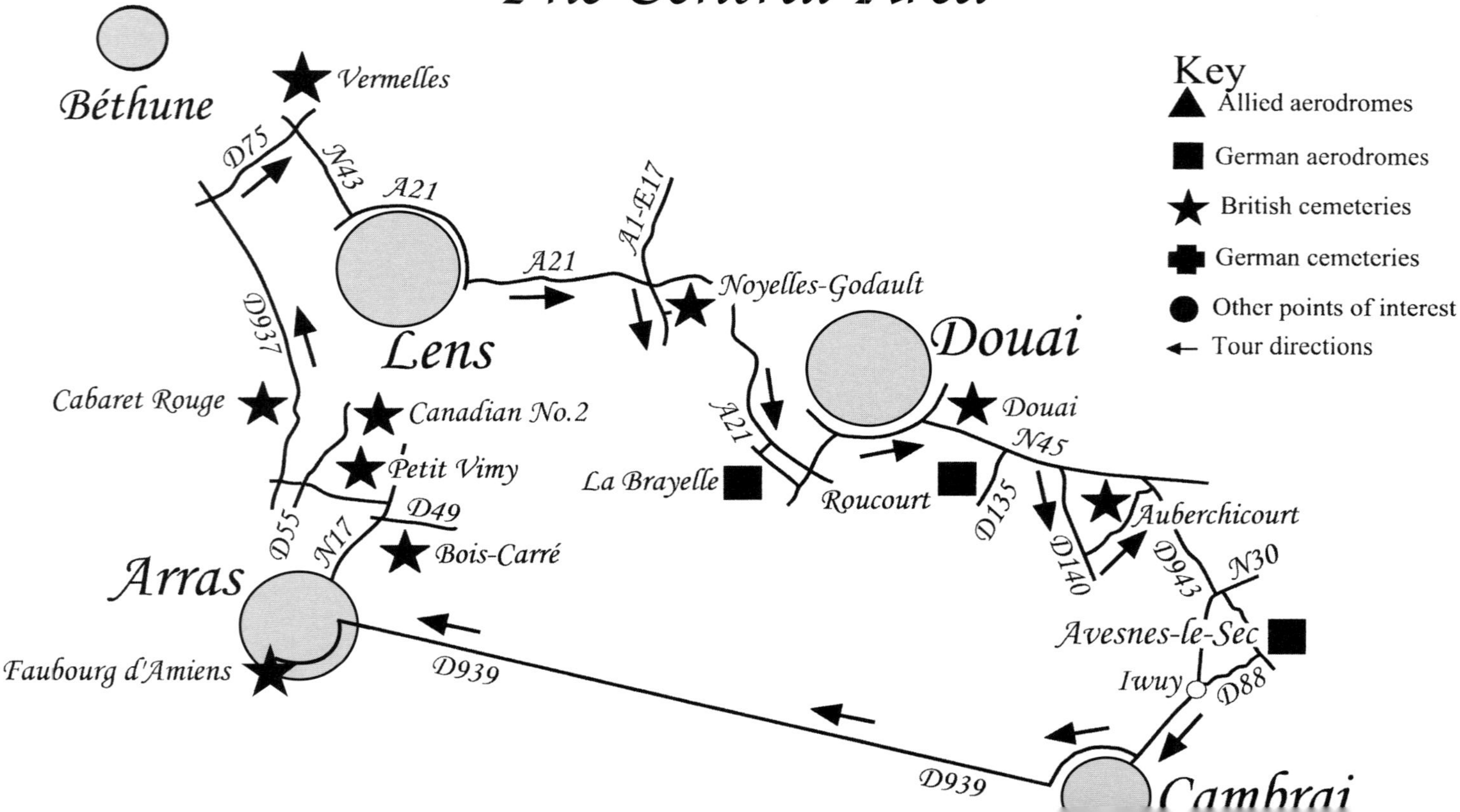

Key
- ▲ Allied aerodromes
- ■ German aerodromes
- ★ British cemeteries
- ✚ German cemeteries
- ● Other points of interest
- ← Tour directions

Béthune

Vermelles

Cabaret Rouge

Lens

N43 A21

D75

D937

D55

N17

D49

Petit Vimy

Canadian No.2

Bois-Carré

Arras

Faubourg d'Amiens

A21

A1-E17

Noyelles-Godault

Douai

N45

Douai

D135

D140

D943

D30

Auberchicourt

Avesnes-le-Sec

Iwuy

D88

Roucourt

La Brayelle

A21

D939

D939

Cambrai

Chapter Two

THE CENTRAL AREA

This chapter covers von Richthofen's activities in the Lens, Douai and Arras areas, including his *Jasta* 11 period at Roucourt and his early career with *Jasta* 2 at La Brayelle.

Bois-Carré Military Cemetery – Four casualties from 16 Squadron
Petit Vimy British Cemetery – E A Welch and A G Tollervey
Canadian Cemetery No. 2 Neuville-St-Vaast – 25 Squadron
Cabaret Rouge British Cemetery – 2 and 43 Squadrons
Vermelles British Cemetery – G W B Hampton 2 Squadron
Noyelles-Godault Communal Cemetery – 25 Squadron
La Brayelle German Aerodrome – Command of *Jasta* 11
Douai Communal Cemetery – H D K George 48 Squadron
Roucourt German Aerodrome – *Jasta* 11 and Bloody April
Auberchicourt British Cemetery – R W Farquhar 32 Squadron
Avesnes-le-Sec German Aerodrome – *Jagdgeschwader* I
Faubourg d'Amiens – The Air Forces Memorial to the Missing

Leave Arras on the N17. Pass under the motorway. At the next traffic lights turn right on the D49 to Thélus Centre. Go through the village and the cemetery is on the right.

Bois-Carré Military Cemetery

This area was taken by Canadian troops on 9 April 1917, and remained in Allied hands for the rest of the war. First begun during the Battle of Arras, the cemetery was used until June 1918, by which time there were 61 graves. It was greatly enlarged after the war and now there are over 500 burials in the cemetery. Additionally there are a small number of Second World War graves. On either side of the Cross of Sacrifice are Duhallow Memorials to those who were buried in other cemeteries whose graves were later lost, including those from the quaintly named Bumble Trench Cemetery.

There are eight RFC graves, four men from 16 Squadron, two from 25 Squadron and two from 59 Squadron.

The pilot of the 25 Squadron FE is another decorated ace of the First World War, Lancelot L Richardson MC. He was Australian and with his various observers had accounted for seven hostile aircraft between June 1916 and March 1917. He was killed on 13 April, shot down by Hans Klein of *Jasta* 4.

The cemetery contains two crews shot down by von Richthofen, Murray and McRae are in Plot I, near the entrance, in the fourth row from the back, while MacKenzie and Everingham are beyond in Plot III, in the centre of the second row from the rear.

Percy William Murray (I D 1/2) and **Duncan John McRae** (I D 1/2)

Lieutenants P W Murray and D J McRae, were yet another crew from the unfortunate 16 Squadron shot down by the Baron on 1 February 1917 for his 19th victory. They had taken off from Bruay at 1430 hours on a Photographic Operation over Thélus. Just forty minutes later they were attacked by von Richthofen, the aircraft descending in large, uncontrolled right hand turns until it crashed into the German front line wire. Both occupants were alive when pulled from the aircraft but each died of his wounds shortly afterwards. Although the aircraft was reported to have landed under control, so may not have been too badly damaged, it was totally destroyed by shell fire some twenty minutes later.

Percy Murray, the son of Mr and Mrs W A Murray of 10 Claremont Terrace, Norton on Tees, Country Durham, was born in 1896. He had been educated at Armstrong College, Newcastle, and was studying Mechanical Engineering at Durham University as the war began.

Lieutentant P W Murray, 16 Squadron, killed in action, 1 February 1917.

He immediately volunteered for service and was gazetted second lieutenant with the 6/Durham Light Infantry and arrived in France with them on 17 April 1915, being made temporary lieutenant on 5 November. Pitched into the fighting of Second Ypres, his battalion suffered such heavy losses that it was combined with the 8th Battalion and existed for quite some time as the 6/8 Durham Light Infantry before sufficient replacements could be found for each to return to their former identities.

Murray then transferred to the RFC and completed his pilot training, being appointed a flying officer on 20 October 1916.

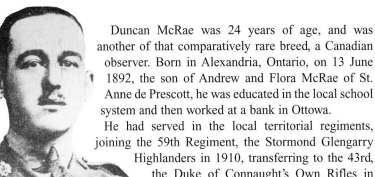

Duncan McRae was 24 years of age, and was another of that comparatively rare breed, a Canadian observer. Born in Alexandria, Ontario, on 13 June 1892, the son of Andrew and Flora McRae of St. Anne de Prescott, he was educated in the local school system and then worked at a bank in Ottowa.

He had served in the local territorial regiments, joining the 59th Regiment, the Stormond Glengarry Highlanders in 1910, transferring to the 43rd, the Duke of Connaught's Own Rifles in 1912. In August 1915 he attested for overseas service with the 77th Battalion Canadian Expeditionary Force and sailed with them from Halifax, Nova Scotia on 19 July 1916.

Duncan McRae finally arrived in France on 11 August 1916, having transferred to the 50th Battalion (Alberta Regiment) CEF. On 19

Lieutentant D J McRae, 16 Squadron, killed in action, 1 February 1917.

December he moved again this time to the RFC – the same month in which one of his brothers was killed in the trenches.

McRae was not Murray's usual observer, but was filling in for W J Lidsey (see page 44) when they were both killed.

Keith Ingelby MacKenzie (III B 12) and Guy Everingham (III B 13)

Second Lieutenants MacKenzie and Everingham also of 16 Squadron, became von Richthofen's 39th victory on 8 April 1917, his second victory of the day. He had already shot down a Sopwith 1½ Strutter of 43 Squadron near Farbus the same morning. (see page 168)

MacKenzie and Everingham had taken off at 1500 hours on a photographic mission to make a photo mosaic of Farbus, just a few hours before the Allied offensive was about to begin. Perhaps they were concentrating too much on their work, because at 1640 hours they had their BE2g shot to pieces in the air during a surprise attack by the Baron, the wreckage falling near Vimy on the German side of the lines. The extent of the break up of their machine can be judged by the fact that

49

Second Lieutenant K I MacKenzie, 16 Squadron, killed in action, 8 April 1917, aged 18.

in his combat report von Richthofen reported that the wreckage was spread over more than a kilometre!

Falling into a battle area, their bodies were not buried immediately but were discovered some days later by advancing Allied troops near Bois de Bonval.

Born on 26 June 1898, Keith MacKenzie was the son of K W I and Florence MacKenzie of 'Lansdowne House', Ryde, Isle of Wight. Keith seems to have followed his Scottish roots rather than his birthplace, when he was gazetted as a second lieutenant in the Argyll and Sutherland Highlanders in April 1916, still two months short of his eighteenth birthday.

Just a month later, on 17 May 1916 he was awarded his Royal Aero Club Aviator's Certificate, number 2906, and shortly afterwards was attached to the Royal Flying Corps. He was the youngest of von Richthofen's victims and only eighteen when he died.

Guy Everingham was the elder son of William and Patricia Florence Everingham of 'Vaenor', Hawarden Road, Colwyn Bay, Denbighshire in North Wales, although he had been born in the south of that country, at Barry, Glamorgan on 28 June 1894.

Educated privately, he joined the 13(1/North Wales) Battalion, the Royal Welsh Fusiliers in October 1914. Picked out as officer material, he was gazetted in the same regiment as a second lieutenant on 25 February 1915. Arriving in France in March 1916, Guy served first in the line, then later as a Bombing Officer in the 113th Trench Mortar Battery.

In September 1916 he successfully applied for transfer to the RFC and trained as an observer, and married Gladys Annie Brown at Holy Trinity Church, Llandudno on 19 February 1917. They set up home at 'Lynwood',

22-year-old Second Lieutenant G Everingham, 16 Squadron, killed in action, 8 April 1917.

St. David's Place in Llandudno, Guy enjoyed a short leave before returning to France for duty with 16 Squadron.

Perhaps Guy had not altered the name of his next of kin in his personal details, or the change had not had time to work its way through the system, but for whatever reason the telegram relating news of his death was sent to his mother, who then had to relay the terrible news to her daughter-in-law.

It was the second such telegram Mrs Everingham had received, as her younger son Robin had been killed at Gallipoli on 10 December 1915 while serving as a trooper in the Welsh Horse.

Return to the traffic lights and turn right on the N17 to Lens. Continue down the hill into Vimy. Look for the green CWGC sign on the left. Turn up the side road and look for the green cemetery sign to the right. Park in the road adjacent to the sign and walk up the lane. The cemetery will come into view ahead to the right in the middle of a field.

Petit-Vimy British Cemetery

Like many small cemeteries on the Western Front, Petit-Vimy has a very intimate atmosphere, accentuated by its isolation and its views to the east from its position half way up the face of Vimy Ridge.

Begun in May 1917, it was used until the October, then enlarged after the war with graves from the battlefields to the north-west. Even after this 'enlargement' there are only 94 graves, of whom 23 are unidentified.

The vast majority of the graves display the Canadian maple leaf. In comparison, the graves we have come to visit are those of the only two RFC men here. They are in the top row, with their backs to the wall supporting the Cross of Sacrifice, and almost directly below it.

Eric Arthur Welch (A 5) and Amos George Tollervy (A 4)

Second Lieutenant E A Welch and Sergeant A G Tollervy, another crew from the long-suffering 16 Squadron, were the Baron's 47th victory, scored on 23 April 1917, two more victims of that bloody month.

They had taken off with another BE2f at around 0930 hours, on a Photographic Operation to the east of Vimy. Some two and a half hours later the two BE2s were attacked by five hostile aircraft, one being shot down by Manfred von Richthofen, and the second by his brother Lothar some five minutes later to become his tenth victim.

Welch and Tollervy probably never knew what hit them, as the Baron managed to approach them unnoticed and opened fire at close range. The BE lost a left wing during the attack and then broke up in the air as it plummeted down over Méricourt.

Eric Welch was born in London in 1894 but was living with his parents Mr and Mrs A T Welch at 1 Belle Vue Terrace, Lancaster when war came. The family must have moved north some years earlier, as Eric had received at least some of his education at Lancaster Royal Grammar School, later being apprenticed as a motor engineer with Atkinson and Sons, lorry manufacturers in Bedford.

He immediately joined up at the beginning of the war, and served in the ranks before receiving a commission as a second lieutenant in 10/(Reserve) Battalion, The King's Own Royal Lancaster Regiment, later being posted to the 7th Battalion. With no sign of going to France, he transferred to the RFC and became a pilot. Following his training he was first posted to 53 Squadron and had only joined No.16 a few days before being shot down.

Amos Tollervey was born on 9 March 1896, and had lived at his family home, 19 Bawtry Road, New Cross, Clifton Hill, London, SE14. Educated locally, his aptitude for engineering secured him his first job at a gun shop in the City of London. When war broke out he volunteered, but unable to follow his brother Alfred into the Royal Navy joined the Royal Flying Corps in January 1915 as a mechanic.

He did very well in the service, and showed an aptitude for photography so that he worked his way quickly up through the ranks and became a Sergeant Observer. He had been already wounded in an earlier action, although not seriously enough to qualify as a 'Blighty' wound, requiring removal to England for treatment.

Sergeant A G Tollervey, observer to Second Lieutenant E A Welch, 16 Squadron, both killed in action, 23 April 1917.

On 23 April 1917 Tollervey should have been back in England on leave but he had taken the place of another Sergeant Observer whose wife was about to give birth.

BE2 A3062 photographed in England before delivery to the RFC. On 23 April 1917 Second Lieutenant E A Welch and Sergeant A Tollervey became von Richthofen's 47th victory.

Return to the N17 and continue back up the hill towards Arras. At the top of the hill turn right on the D55E2 to the Canadian Memorial. At the T junction go right on the D55 to Givenchy and then turn left at the CWGC sign to the cemetery.

Canadian Cemetery No. 2, Neuville-St-Vaast

The cemetery is located within the area set aside as the Canadian National Vimy Memorial Park, and during the last part of the journey from Neuville-St-Vaast village you are surrounded by forested areas on either side of the road. The trees tend to hide the broken nature of the ground, which has been left undisturbed since the end of hostilities.

But the park still leaves an indelible impression of the type of ground the troops had to fight over, even though the trees, the grass and eighty plus years of weathering have rounded out the craters.

The park is dominated by the huge Canadian memorial, but also contains an area of preserved trenches and one of the tunnels used to enable the troops to get to the front line ready to attack Vimy Ridge on 9 April 1917, the opening day of the Battle of Arras. All are worth a visit if time permits.

This cemetery was begun after the Canadian Corps' successful attack, and some of the graves are of those who were killed or died of their wounds here at the time, though the majority of the burials are of the dead brought in from the surrounding battlefields and from isolated graves for some years after the armistice.

Today there are almost 3,000 graves here, well over half of whom are unidentified. Perhaps because of its name and its location within the Memorial Park, the Canadian nature of the cemetery is reinforced by a small maple leaf on the entrance gate, and by a non-standard Visitors Book printed in French and English.

Within such a large total there are just four airmen. Apart from Arthur Boultbee and Frederick King, to whom we have come to pay our respects today, are Second Lieutenants F E Hollingsworth and H M W Wells, the crew of an 11 Squadron FE2b, killed on 15 September 1916 during the Battle of Flers-Courcelette.

The graves of Boultbee and King are in Plot XI. Walk down the central aisle and plot XI is on the left, immediately beyond the pathway between the Cross of Sacrifice and the shelter containing the cemetery register. Graves A1 and A2 are the first two graves in the front row.

Arthur Elsdale Boultbee (XI A 2) and **Frederick King** (XI A 1)

The graves are those of two men who became the Baron's victory number 27 on 17 March 1917, a day during which he would also gain his 28th victory, shooting down Watt and Howlett of 16 Squadron in the afternoon. (see page 39)

Boultbee and King were with 25 Squadron flying FE2b 'pushers' and on the morning of the 17th had taken of at 0900 hours with an escort of 43 Squadron's Sopwith 1¹/₂ Strutters during a photo-reconnaissance sortie. It was quite a large formation for the period, nine FEs (three carrying cameras) and nine 1¹/₂ Strutters.

About an hour and a half later von Richthofen led nine of his *staffel* into the attack, (although his combat report quotes only 15 British machines). The British FEs had begun to circle for mutual defence, but von Richthofen managed to force his victim out of formation, then concentrated on it, his fire cutting the rear booms from the forward gondola and wings. Once again the crew had no chance of surviving the fall of their disintegrating FE near Oppy.

Arthur Boultbee was born in St Ives, Huntingdonshire in 1897, but by the time of the First World War he was living with his parents, Reverend

Lieutenant A E Boultbee, 25 Squadron, killed in action 17 March 1917.

Frederick Croxall Boultbee and his wife Henrietta at The Rectory, Hargrave, Northamptonshire. Educated at St. John's, Leatherhead, he was awarded an Exhibition in History worth £25 and went up to St. Catherine's College Cambridge. However, he only completed one term before joining up.

Originally commissioned into the Northamptonshire's, his county regiment, he transferred to the RFC and after pilot training joined 25 Squadron in 1 January 1917, lasting just ten weeks.

A photograph of Boultbee's body was sent to von Richthofen with

Air Mechanic Second Class F King, Boultbee's observer, 25 Squadron.

the following message written on the back:

To Baron Manfred von Richthofen: Sir, I witnessed on 17 March 1917 your air fight, and took this photograph, which I send to you with hearty congratulations, because you seldom have the occasion to see your prey. Vivat Sequens! (Here's to the next!). With Fraternal Greetings, Baron von Riezenstein, Colonel and Commandant of the Eighty-Seventh Reserve Regiment.

Frederick King was born and raised in Deeping St. Nicholas, Spalding, Lincolnshire where he lived with his parents Tim and Florence. Educated at the local Middle Township School, he then volunteered for his county regiment, the Lincolnshires.

Picked for transfer to the Royal Flying Corps, he completed his training as an observer and was eventually posted to 25 Squadron. After his death his mother learned that he was being considered for a commission at the time of his death.

Return to the D55, turn left and continue to Neuville-St-Vaast. In the centre of the village go right on the D49 Autres Directions. Turn right on the D937 to Carency Souchez. Continue ahead and the cemetery is on the right.

Cabaret Rouge British Cemetery

On 26 September 1915 this area was taken from the Germans by the French, although the village of Souchez a mile to the north was completely destroyed. They in turn handed over in March 1916 to Commonwealth forces who occupied this sector. The level of French commitment in the area can be seen in the graveyard and Chapel of Notre Dame de Lorette visible to the north from the cemetery, containing the French unknown soldiers from various conflicts throughout the twentieth century.

The 'Cabaret Rouge' was a house just south of the village, the word *cabaret* in French referring to a building housing a number of small businesses. The concept of something made up of different parts then gave its name to the more familiar form of entertainment which we know today.

On the east side opposite the cemetery grounds were dugouts that were used as battalion headquarters in 1916. Various communication trenches ended here, one of which was named after the Cabaret, so perhaps it was the trench and not the original building which gave its name to the cemetery.

The cemetery was used between March 1916 and August 1917 and then at intervals until September 1918. Of the 7,655 Commonwealth burials, more than 7,000 were concentrated here after the war from the battlefields of Arras, and from 103 other burial sites in the Nord and Pas de Calais, more than half the burials are unidentified. There is a single Second World War burial.

For a cemetery of its size it has an attractive layout, unlike some of the larger concentration ones which tend to have the graves arranged in row after row. There are some unusual burials here. Visit grave VIII E 7, at about 11 o'clock from the Stone of Remembrance, and you will see that in a row of Canadian unknowns, one headstone is inscribed to show that on 25 May 2000 the body within was exhumed by staff of the Commonwealth War Graves Commission and in a special ceremony entrusted to Canada to become their Unknown Soldier and now lies in Ottawa.

Another unusual group, with a flying context, can be found in Plot XV, to the left of the Canadian Unknown, in graves XV G 22, 23 and 24. As Mike O'Connor has mentioned in *Airfields and Airmen, Arras*, one of the questions regularly asked is why RFC as well as RAF headstones only display the RAF badge. Occasionally, you do encounter RFC headstones but they a far less common.

Of the known graves, 79 are airmen, including twelve from 25 Squadron and ten from 43 Squadron. There are two British aces, Arthur Claydon DFC of 32 Squadron, (grave number VII E 6), killed in action in July 1918, shot down by Paul Billik of *Jasta* 52, and William G S Curphey MC & Bar also of 32 Squadron, (grave number XVI G 8), killed in action in May 1917. He was shot down by Franz Walz, leader of *Jasta* 2.

Of the aircrew in the cemetery, there are several victims of the Red Baron and the first one we have come to pay our respects to is Herbert Croft who is buried in Plot VII to the right of the central aisle.

Herbert Arthur Croft (VII H 11)

Lieutenant Herbert Croft, observer, and Second Lieutenant C D Bennett, pilot, were flying their BE2d of 2 Squadron when they became victory number 20 for von Richthofen on the late morning of 14 February 1917, the first of two victories he would gain that day.

They had left their airfield at Hesdigneul, near Béthune, about an hour and a half earlier, and were engaged on artillery observation – or Art Obs – when the Baron caught them west of Loos around noon. Von Richthofen, who was returning from a meeting at *Jasta Boelcke*, edged towards the front lines to see if anything was happening.

He spotted the BE and closed in unnoticed, getting as close as 50 metres before the British crew saw him due no doubt to their preoccupation with the job in hand. They had already been ranging the 186th Siege Battery for an hour and after the red plane dived on them, observers on the ground saw the BE spiral down over Cité St Auguste.

Second Lieutenant C D Bennett of 2 Squadron, prisoner of war on 14 February 1917. Born in Moscow and then living with his family in Riga, just after WW1 he served against the Bolsheviks with 47 Squadron.

Herbert Arthur Croft had either been killed in the air by the Baron's gunfire or died soon after being taken from the wreck. It seems doubly tragic that although Herbert Croft paid the supreme sacrifice, none of his personal records exist.

Cyril Bennett suffered injuries so severe that afterwards he could not remember any details of his last flight or the name of his observer, and was unconscious for two days in a German field hospital in Carvin. He was a prisoner until being repatriated on 6 December 1918.

Bennett had been born in Moscow, Russia, where his British father had a business. Despite the fact that his health was still less than perfect almost two years after his crash, Bennett immediately volunteered for service against the Bolsheviks. His worth as a Russian speaker was recognized, and in March 1919 he joined 47 Squadron in South Russia, remaining with the squadron until the evacuation.

57

James Smyth (XII E 9) and **Edward Gordon Byrne** (XII E 8)

The graves of James Smyth and Edward Byrne are immediately to your right as you enter the cemetery, in the next to back row of Plot XII.

Second Lieutenants James Smyth and Edward Byrne were the crew of another BE2d of 2 Squadron, who became the Baron's 26th victory on 11 March 1917, just four weeks after their colleagues Croft and Bennett. Von Richthofen had become separated from his *staffel* but had stalked the BE2d for some time before getting into a favourable position to attack. He fired 200 shots at the BE, which was engaged in a photographic operation near Givenchy, and saw it snap in two leaving the British crew no chance of survival. It fell smoking into the German lines near the forest of La Folie to the west of Vimy.

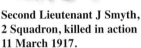

Second Lieutenant J Smyth, 2 Squadron, killed in action 11 March 1917.

James Smyth was born in the Ballymacarrett district of Belfast but his family moved to Kent when he was a youngster as his father was seeking work in the rope and hemp industry. By the outbreak of war, he was married, and lived with his wife,

The great disadvantage of the BE2 series of machines was that the gunner/observer sat in front of the pilot giving him a very limited field of fire.

Edith Martha, and their two children at 'Mossvale', 98 Chestnut Road, Plumstead, Kent.

Although his job with the Borough Engineering Company of London gave him exemption from war service, despite the efforts of his employers to deter him he insisted on joining the RFC. His maturity and engineering background soon picked him out as officer material and following the usual training he was sent out to the front as a pilot with 2 Squadron.

Edward Byrne was 35 years old at the time of his death. Born in 1881, he has the dubious distinction of being the oldest of von Richthofen's victims. Brought up in an orphanage in Edinburgh, and educated at St. Joseph's College, Dumfries, he had followed the path of many other orphans and joined the army as soon as he was old enough. He had spent twelve years in the RAMC, serving in China, India and Africa, retiring from the army some four years before war broke out.

By 1914 he was living in Edinburgh, managing the home and estate of a prominent local businessman, but immediately volunteered for war service. Initially in France with the Australian Volunteer Hospital Corps, which qualified him for the Mons Star, Byrne bored of his duties and applied for transfer to the Duke of Westminster's Armoured Car Squadron, then also in France.

Because of the static nature of the fighting on the Western Front it was decided to send the squadron to the Middle East, but before leaving, the Duke personally recommended Byrne for a commission. Gazetted to the 4/Gordon Highlanders he served in the trenches until severely wounded.

Second Lieutenant E Byrne, 2 Squadron, 35-year old observer to James Smyth, 11 March 1917.

After recovery from his wounds he again applied for a transfer, this time to the RFC. After completing the necessary training Byrne was posted to 'C' Flight, 2 Squadron and his fateful meeting with the Red Baron.

Herbert John Green (XII E 3) and **Alexander William Reid** (XII E 4)

The graves of Herbert Green and Alexander Reid lie just to the left of Smyth and Byrne.

Second Lieutenants Herbert Green and Alexander Reid were the crew of a 43 Squadron 1½ Strutter which became von Richthofen's 23rd victory on 4 March 1917. The Sopwiths of 43 Squadron had taken off from Treizennes, just south of Aire, at 1340 hours to patrol south of Vimy. Just over an hour and a half later they were engaged by six aircraft from *Jasta* 11 over Acheville, and one of the Sopwiths was seen to leave the safety of the group and attack the German fighters, three of which then proceeded to attack it in turn. After some time a wing came off the British aircraft and it fell to the ground.

Second Lieutenant H J Green, 43 Squadron, aged 19. Killed in action 4 March 1917.

'Bertie' Green was born in East Rudham, Norfolk on 30 July 1897, but at the age of nine the family moved back to Newcastle upon Tyne. Four years later he won a scholarship to St. Cuthbert's Grammar School where he shone academically, especially in the sciences. He then continued his education at Armstrong College, and intended to take a degree in science.

He had already joined the Durham University OTC, and volunteered as soon as he was old enough. After training with the Officer Cadet Corps Battalion at Oxford he was gazetted second lieutenant in the Royal Flying Corps on 6 July 1916. He graduated from the Central Flying School, Upavon, on 15 November 1916, and spent what would be his last Christmas at home before crossing to France on 17 January 1917.

There were four Green brothers in the RFC. One, Ernest, was awarded the MC with 16 Squadron but was shot down by *Jasta* 2 on 3 February 1918, whilst serving with 25 Squadron. He survived the war, but was killed in a flying accident at Digby, Lincolnshire on 24 May 1922.

Alex Reid, the son of Captain J J and Mrs F E Reid of 'St Heliers', Denzil Avenue, Southampton, was born in 1896. He had joined the Hampshire Yeomanry as a trooper in 1913, and immediately volunteered for foreign service when war broke out. He was soon commissioned into the 6/King's Own Scottish Borderers as a replacement after the battalion had suffered heavy casualties during the Battle of Loos in September 1915.

Wounded while in the trenches on 1 May 1916, Reid returned to England, and following recovery from his wounds he applied for a

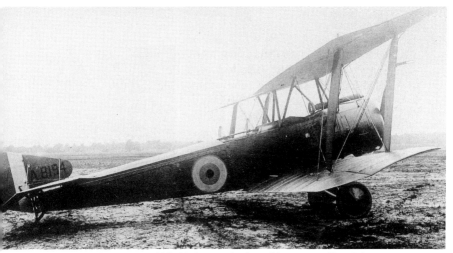

Sopwith 1½ Strutter A8194. Units employing this type suffered heavy casualties as it was easy prey for German fighters.

transfer to the RFC. After training as an observer at Reading and Hythe he returned to France and joined 43 Squadron on 23 February 1917.

Bertie Green had been with 43 Squadron for about six weeks at the time of his death, Alex Reid just nine days. The two were nineteen and twenty years old respectively.

Reuel Dunn (XV M 24)

Dunn is in Plot XV, at about ten o'clock from the Stone of Remembrance, second from the left-hand end of the row, in the last but one row from the back.

Sergeant Reuel Dunn, also of 43 Squadron, was killed on 2 April 1917 as victory number 33, although his pilot, Second Lieutenant A P Warren survived as a wounded prisoner. It was the Baron's second kill of the day, having already despatched Powell and Bonner's 13 Squadron BE2d at 08.35 hours that morning over Farbus village. (They are commemorated on the Arras memorial.)

Algy Warren and Reuel Dunn were in one of six Sopwith 1½ Strutters out on a photo-operation east of Vimy in the late morning, and the Baron met them along with his brother Lothar and Werner Voss. Warren and Dunn were last seen spiralling down into some clouds, the Baron reporting too that the British pilot tried to hide in cloud, but that he had followed

Sergeant R Dunn, Warren's observer on 2 April, and mortally wounded.

them through it and attacked once more.

The Sopwith's fuel tank had been holed and was streaming petrol which forced Warren to get down as quickly as possible. He made a reasonable landing and the Baron had swooped low over them, and later said that the gunner had continued to fire up at his Albatros. Richthofen had then made an attacking run on the downed two-seater, killing one of the occupants – Dunn.

Later Warren was to report that Dunn had been wounded in the air and was in no position to open fire on the German fighter, having been wounded in the abdomen, and that the Albatros attacked them after they had vacated the machine. Dunn died six hours later in a German dressing station. Richthofen gives a slightly different account in his book, which was obviously heavily edited in his favour.

Reuel Dunn was 24 years old and had originally come from Workington, although at the outbreak of war he was living in lodgings in Newcastle upon Tyne where he worked as a ship's architect with Swan, Hunter and Whitworth.

Second Lieutenant A P Warren, 43 Squadron, taken prisoner 2 April 1917.

He enlisted in 1915 and served in France as a despatch rider with the Army Service Corps. His next duties were with a transport column, but he then decided on a change, and successfully applied for transfer to the Royal Flying Corps. After observer training, he saw service with 70 Squadron in 1916 before being posted to 43 Squadron.

Algernon Warren came from Wallingford, Oxfordshire and was nineteen when he was shot down. Educated at Westminster School and Magdelen College, Oxford, his studies were interrupted by the war, when he joined the RFC on 8 July 1916. He saw service as an observer with 57 Squadron before transferring to 34 Reserve Squadron for training as a pilot. Graduating on 3 February 1917 he was sent to 43 Squadron three weeks later.

Following the encounter with von Richthofen, he spent the rest of the war as a prisoner before being repatriated on 17 December 1918. He returned to his studies in Oxford and graduated in 1921, winning the Beit Prize in Colonial History. He subsequently qualified as an architect in 1936, and during the Second World War served as a captain in the Royal Engineers. He died at the family home in Cholsey in 1979 at the age of eighty-one.

Continue north on the D937 and turn right on the D75 to Vermelles (there is a small Eiffel Tower in the centre of the roundabout). Follow the D75 through Mazingarbe. At a roundabout cross over the N43 and continue ahead to the cemetery on your left.

Vermelles British Cemetery

This is a very unusual cemetery, as it is in two completely separate sections, with a side road passing between them, the plot numbers continuing into the section beyond the road. Indeed the grave we have come to see is in this separate, rear section, and the register is to be found just through the gateway into the larger, front section. Another oddity is that the cemetery contains a local shrine, one of the normal roadside chapels seen throughout this part of France, which now stands towards the front of the front plot surrounded by headstones.

The area was originally held by the Germans until December 1914, when it was recovered by the French. The cemetery was begun in August 1915 and during the Battle of Loos the burial area, Plot I, was laid out and fenced by pioneers of the 1/Gloucester Regiment. For a long time afterwards it was known as 'The Gloucester Graveyard'. Later it was used by other divisions holding the line just a mile to the east until it was closed in April 1917. After the armistice further burials took place from the various battlefields to the east, so that today there are over 2,000 burials, of which nearly 200 are unidentified.

Just three of the graves are airmen. We have come to pay our respects to George Hampton, whose grave is in the rear section, beyond the road, in the centre of the first row of graves to the right of the gate.

Interestingly one of the others, John Clark Simpson of 32 Squadron (grave number IV F 24), was killed in the action during which Major Lionel W B Rees MC earned the Victoria Cross on 1 July 1916 – the First Day of the Battle of the Somme.

George William Betts Hampton (V A 26)

For many years von Richthofen's 21st victory was thought to be a Morane Parasol of 3 Squadron crewed by Lieutenant Thomas S Green and Second Lieutenant W K Carse who were both killed. In the last few years it has become apparent that this was an attempt to make evidence fit the facts, and further research has shown that the victims were Captain George Bailey and Second Lieutenant George Hampton of 2 Squadron, flying an BE2c on Artillery Observation duty with 24th Division Artillery over Loos.

Although the timing and location fit with von Richthofen's combat report, one discrepancy remains in that he reported the aircraft as having crashed, and seeing a heavy cloud of smoke in the snow, although he does admit that it was foggy and was already getting rather dark. In fact the BE2 survived the action, although the aircraft was badly shot about, with Bailey reporting bullets through its fuselage, wings and his own seat. Indeed Bailey had been wounded in the knee during the fight. Whether the smoke was caused by the fire from the gun batteries being directed by Bailey and Hampton we will never know.

Captain G C Bailey DSO, narrowly avoided death on 14 February 1917. Although he and his observer survived, he became the Baron's 21st victory.

Although George Hampton survived the combat with the Baron on 14 February 1917, he did not last long after the encounter, being killed in action with another pilot less than a month later, on 11 March, probably shot down by one of von Richthofen's *Jasta* 11 protégés, Karl Schäfer. His pilot, Second Lieutenant G C Hoskins is buried in the next grave, V A 25.

Like Geoffrey Brichta in Barlin, George Hampton was somewhat older than his fellow officers, being aged 31 at the time of his death. Born in 1886, he lived with his wife Violet at 7 St. Mary Road, Walthamstow, Essex. At the outbreak of war he volunteered immediately and became a private soldier in the 1/4 Cameron Highlanders, crossing to France with them on 15 February 1915.

Selected for officer training, he was commissioned into the 3/5

Suffolk Regiment, but became bored with life in a training/feeder battalion and successfully applied for a transfer to the Royal Flying Corps, soon afterwards finding himself in France as an observer with 2 Squadron.

George Bailey recovered from the wounds he received during the action with von Richthofen, and indeed survived the war. He received the DSO in July 1917 (for an action which predated his meeting with the Baron), and after recovery from his wounds he returned to the Western Front in command of 57 Squadron.

Offered a permanent commission after the end of hostilities, he remained in the Royal Air Force and served in India and Iraq, also attending Staff College at Andover in 1925. By the outbreak of the Second World War he was an air commodore, and was appointed Director of Equipment at the Air Ministry until his retirement in 1944, when he received a CBE. He died in Honiton, Devon in 1972 in his eighty-second year.

Return to the N43 and turn left for Lens. Turn on to the A21 towards Paris and Lille and follow A21 A1 Paris signs. Immediately after turning on the A1 leave at junction 17 for Noyelles-Godault. At the traffic lights go left signposted Centre Ville and pass under the motorway. At the first roundabout go right to Courrières and Oignies then follow the D160E1 to the A21. After leaving the village the cemetery comes in to view down a side road to the right.

Noyelles-Godault Communal Cemetery

On entering the civilian cemetery turn immediately to the left, and the row of five graves will be seen on the left-hand side of the path, with their backs to a laurel hedge. Four of the five are fliers, with those of Bates and Barnes being the first and second respectively. Bates's headstone carries the moving epitaph *'His sun went down while it was day'*.

Allan Harold Bates and William Alfred Barnes

This is another Bloody April crew, Second Lieutenant A H Bates and Sergeant W A Barnes, flying an FE2b of 25 Squadron. They were von Richthofen's third kill of the day, taking his total of victories to forty-three. In the morning of 13 April 1917 he had shot down a 59 Squadron RE8, (see page 168) and then earlier in the afternoon had brought down another FE2b, of 11 Squadron. (see page 168)

Bates and Barnes were one of a formation of six FEs which had taken off at 1840 hours to bomb an ammunition dump between Henin-Liétard and Lens. Soon after they had completed their bombing they saw five scouts approaching. They looked like Nieuports, and as Captain J L Leith in charge of the mission had been advised that these machines were in the area they did not open fire.

In fact they were *Jasta* 11 and *Jasta* 4, led by von Richthofen, and their hostile nature was revealed when they swooped down and attacked the formation, shooting down two of the FEs straightaway, and a third shortly afterwards. Bates and Barnes were seen to be gliding down under control, and at first it was hoped that they might have survived to be taken prisoner, but their aircraft hit a house in Noyelles-Godault and both were killed.

Presumably they were buried in the local cemetery at the time, and after the war it was decided for whatever reason that they should remain there, rather than be concentrated into a War Graves Commission cemetery, as happened in most cases.

Allan Bates hailed from Swansea, the son of Archibald and Harriett Elizabeth Bates, of 'The Utility Stores', 44 St. Helens Road. Born in May 1896, he received his early education at the local school near to the family shop, which sold hardware and electrical goods.

From school he went to the local technical college, and then worked in an aeroplane factory before being accepted for the RFC. After training at the Officer Cadet Training Battalion based at Lincoln College, Oxford he was gazetted a second lieutenant in the RFC, and following further training was awarded his wings.

Victory No.43 on 13 April 1917, was a 25 Squadron crew, Second Lieutenant A H Bates, a month short of his 21st birthday.

His first job as a pilot was ferrying aircraft to St. Omer, the main supply depot in France. He was posted to 25 Squadron exactly one week before falling to the guns of the Baron's Albatros DIII.

William Barnes was the son of Chief Warder William and Mrs Edith Barnes and was born in 1885. His father had been a professional soldier before entering the prison service, or 'Convict

Bates' observer was 31-years old Sergeant W A Barnes MSM, buried beside his pilot in Noyelles-Godault cemetery.

Service' as it was known at the time, and William followed in his father's footsteps, joining the Army Service Corps in 1901, seeing service in Egypt and the Sudan.

The war found him back in England and he was in France by early October with the 7th Division, qualifying him for the Mons Star. Continued good work with the corps resulted in the award of the Meritorious Service Medal on 18 October 1916.

After several attempts, he was finally successful in transferring to the RFC, and after the appropriate period received his observer's wing in November 1916. He enjoyed a short leave with his family, his parents, his two brothers and his sister, on the Isle of Wight, where his father was working at Parkhurst Prison. He joined 25 Squadron on 1 April 1917, just two weeks before his death, thereby serving one week longer than his pilot.

Return to the D160E1 and turn right. At the roundabout go right towards the A21. At the next roundabout turn left for the A21. Turn almost immediately left on to the A21 to Douai. Continue on the motorway and after junction 18 follow Cambrai signs. Leave the motorway at the Usine Renault sign. At the traffic lights turn left for the A1 to Arras. Stop at the hard shoulder past the factory adjacent to a château.

La Brayelle German Aerodrome

Like a lot of northern France the area is now heavily industrialised and most of this historic site has disappeared under the huge Renault car factory.

Jasta 11 arrived here on 11 October 1916 and von Richthofen was

La Brayelle looking north-east towards Douai across the Renault factory.

posted to command it on 15 January 1917. He was wearing his newly awarded *Pour le Mérite*. Up to his arrival no victories had been claimed but he rectified this when he brought down their first and his seventeenth on 23 January. The victim was John Hay, flying an FE8 of 40 Squadron who was killed. (see page 37)

It was 40 Squadron who were also involved in bringing down von Richthofen on 6 March 1917 – near Henin-Liétard. *Jasta* 11 had been in a scrap with their FE8s that had come to the rescue of the two-seat Sopwiths of 43 Squadron. 40 Squadron claimed two of the German aircraft shot down, one by Captain Robert Gregory, the other by Lieutenant E L Benbow. *Leutnant* Eduard Lübbert's machine was hit

Billet and dug-outs at La Brayelle.

and he was slightly wounded, having to make a forced landing. Von Richthofen's aircraft was badly damaged too and he also needed to make a hurried forced landing, which he did successfully. He came to rest in a small meadow five kilometres from Henin-Liétard, alongside a main road. Unfortunately the exact location has never been identified.

He had been lucky for his petrol tank had been shot through and he went down trailing petrol vapour. Safely down he took time to inspect the damage, seeing both petrol tanks were empty and the engine damaged. He then took a nap with some front line troops in their dugout, had some lunch and then made his way back to his base at Brayelle, which was no more than a six kilometre flight to the south-east.

Von Richthofen in front of a *Jasta* 2 Albatros DII. The binoculars would be used to watch the nearby lines for Allied aircraft prior to take-off.

Von Richthofen scored victories 17 to 43 flying from here, the last being A H Bates and W A Barnes of 25 Squadron who are buried in Noyelles-Godault Communal Cemetery. (see page 66)

But the British had found them and were starting to make their lives

An unusual T-shaped hanger on La Brayelle airfield.

Spad VII A6706, 19 Squadron. Victory No.30 for the Baron, its pilot, Lieutenant R P Baker was taken prisoner.

a misery. RFC night bombers attacked the airfield on the night of the 5/6 April, and again on the night of 7/8th although the main target was Douai railway station, with Brayelle as a secondary objective. Plans to move to another airfield were finalised for the 13th, moving to Roucourt. That night the bombers were back but the airfield was empty.

The new base for *Jasta* 11, was Roucourt south-east of Douai. (see page 74)

Lieutenant R P Baker.

Continue ahead. Follow Douai signs towards the town centre. At the inner ring road turn right for Valenciennes and continue on the N45 towards Valenciennes then turn right on the N45 to Denain. Pass over the railway and the cemetery is on the left.

Douai Communal Cemetery

Douai was briefly in the hands of the Allies in the first weeks of the war, when it was held by the French, and in a rather indirect connection with British aviation, by the Royal Naval Air Service with their armoured cars.

It was taken by the Germans on 1 October 1914, and was to remain in their hands until virtually the end of the war, being liberated on 17

October 1918. No. 42 Casualty Clearing Station was then based in the town until November 1919, but the vast majority of the burials date from the time of the German occupation, as British, French, Russian, Rumanian and Italian prisoners of war were buried here, as well as German troops.

Today there are some 200 First World War graves, of whom twenty are unidentified, and a large number of Second World War graves. The cemetery has a very long and narrow shape, squeezed between the boundary wall of the civilian cemetery and a hedge marking the end of the civilian burials. Because there is no boundary wall, a small brick pillar has been built to the side of the Cross of Sacrifice to hold the register and visitor's book.

There is a large air service contingent in the cemetery – nineteen. Twelve of these are from fighter squadrons, including the victim of von Richthofen we have come to see, Herbert George. His grave is in the row on the right, with its back to the cemetery wall. Numbering starts from the far end of the row, so his grave is the seventh from the far end.

Herbert Duncan King George (D 7)

Second Lieutenant George, who became von Richthofen's thirty-fifth victory on 5 April 1917, was an observer in 48 Squadron, flying in the early Bristol F2a two-seater, his pilot being Second Lieutenant A N Lechler. The squadron was new to the Western Front – indeed George would be its first casualty – as was the Bristol Fighter, and in the beginning they were not used as aggressively as they were later.

If attacked they tended to adopt the normal technique of two-seater crews, which was to circle, relying on the defensive fire from the observers to defend the formation. Later, once correct fighter tactics were employed, they became formidable opponents having realised that the BF2b could dog-fight virtually any enemy fighter that was encountered.

The squadron had a disastrous start to its career on the Western Front. On the morning of 5 April Captain William Leefe Robinson VC led six Bristols of his squadron on their first ever operational flight, conducting an Offensive Patrol towards Douai, and ran into Richthofen's *staffel*. Four Bristols were brought down by *Jasta* 11, and although all crewmen were captured, only George died. The two surviving RFC machines scraped back over the lines shot full of holes, and the Baron later said that his pilots should have no fear from the new British two-seaters. (Leefe Robinson had been awarded the VC for bringing down the German airship SL11 on 3 September 1916 over Cuffley, north-east of London.)

The grave of H D K George. This is a standard Commonwealth War Graves Commission headstone and displays the RAF badge though the RAF was not formed until a year after his death.

Second Lieutenant A N Lechler, 48 Squadron, wounded and taken prisoner on 5 April 1917. This was the Baron's first encounter with the new Bristol F2a two-seat fighter.

Lechler and George came down near Lewarde, south of Douai, George having been seriously wounded in the air. Lechler managed to land the aircraft safely, and to drag his observer clear, despite being wounded himself, and then set fire to the machine. George had received wounds to back and leg and he died in a German hospital the next day.

Herbert George was born in Satara, India on 23 July 1897, the son of Duncan and Florence George, whose home in England was at 7 Stanhope Terrace, Hyde Park, London. He spent his early years in India, and then returned to England to attend his father's old school Clifton College.

He then entered the Royal Military College, Sandhurst, after which he was commissioned into the Royal Dublin Fusiliers on 12 May 1915. Still only seventeen, he was too young for foreign service, and was posted

The Baron's room at Roucourt with his 'trophies' on the wall. Serial number A3340 (centre) was cut from Lechler's Bristol Fighter.

to the regimental depot at Cork until he was able to join the 2nd Battalion in France in 1916. Shortly after his arrival in France he applied for a transfer to the Royal Flying Corps, and returned to England in the July for observer's training. He was posted back to France with 48 Squadron on 8 March 1917.

Arthur Lechler had also been born in India, at Yercaud, Madras, on 13 February 1890, where his father was a coffee planter. The youngest

Bristol F2a A3307. After encountering this type in April 1917 the Baron dismissed them as sub-standard opponents. Later the BF2b became a formidable opponent for German fighter pilots.

of four sons, he returned to England for his education, and was in the second year of a civil engineering degree at Edinburgh University when war broke out. He joined the 9/Royal Scots, known as the 'Dandy Ninth' because they were the only battalion of that regiment to be kilted, the rest wearing 'trews'.

Selected for officer training, he was commissioned into the 15th (Service) Battalion of the Manchester Regiment on 3 March 1915. He then transferred to the RFC, and after completing his pilot training he went back to France with 48 Squadron.

After his capture, Arthur Lechler remained in captivity until 9 April 1918, when he was repatriated via Holland, so that his wounds could be properly treated. After the war he returned to Edinburgh University to complete his degree, and then worked for most of the time in India until the outbreak of the Second World War. He returned to uniform, as a major in the Royal Engineers, based at Edinburgh Castle with Headquarters Scottish Command. He died suddenly on 7 June 1949 aged fifty-nine.

Continue ahead on the N45 and turn right at the roundabout on the D135 to Roucourt. At the stop sign turn right again on the D135 to Roucourt. Pass the church, visible down a side street, then at the next cross roads turn right in to Rue Leon Poutrain. Follow the château wall which is on the left until the corner. On your left is the château and ahead down a track is what was the aerodrome.

Roucourt German Aerodrome

Jasta 11 established itself here on 13 April 1917, arriving from La Brayelle, near Douai. (see page 67) The Battle of Arras had commenced a few days before and there was no shortage of British machines to shoot down. Von Richthofen though was only to claim nine British machines while he was here because on 1 May he handed command of the unit to his brother Lothar and went on leave. However in his absence his pilots claimed some 80 Allied machines. No wonder the RFC called April 1917 'Bloody April'.

Again one can make out the field that made up the flying area, and the château close by is surrounded by a high wall with its ornate garden in front of the building, its wide drive-way leading to the entrance. On page 78 of the old Harleyford book *Von Richthofen and the Flying Circus* published in 1958 (a book exceptionally well done at this early

Roucourt Aerodrome

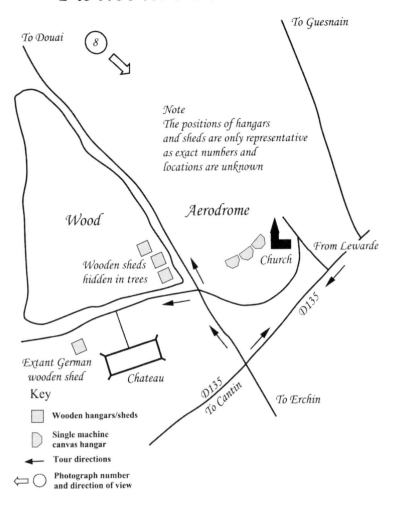

To Douai

(8)

To Guesnain

Note
The positions of hangars
and sheds are only representative
as exact numbers and
locations are unknown

Wood

Aerodrome

Wooden sheds
hidden in trees

Church

From Lewarde

D135

Extant German
wooden shed

Chateau

D135
To Cantin

To Erchin

Key

- ☐ Wooden hangars/sheds
- ◗ Single machine canvas hangar
- ← Tour directions
- ⇐ ◯ Photograph number and direction of view

Photograph No. 8: Roucourt looking roughly south-east in 1999.

ROUCOURT VILLAGE

ROUCOURT CHATEAU

GERMAN SHED

AERODROME

A pre-WW1 picture of the Château de Roucourt. (Note the moulding above the door to the left, below the balustrade).

stage of recording the flying events of the First World War), there is an informal photograph of von Richthofen and Kurt Wolff, one of his *Jasta* 11 aces. Both look as if they have either just returned to the château from a sortie, or are about to depart to the airfield. The picture is captioned as Marcke but this is incorrect as the actual location is Roucourt.

In the background to this photo there is a curved wall with a large stucco decoration above a door. There is still a curved wall there, but the door is different and the wall decoration is no longer in-situ. The present owner of the building confirmed that the château was destroyed by fire in 1918, but after the war it was rebuilt in a similar

The Château today. Virtually destroyed in 1918, it was rebuilt after the First World War to much simpler lines. The left side door is now just an opening into the rear garden and the balustrade above is gone.

Von Richthofen and Wolff outside the château with the moulding on the wall behind them.

Historian Brad King with the present owner of the château, Baron Becquet de Megille, standing approximately where the Baron and Wolff are in the above photo.

style. The curved wall, its door and the stucco decoration were not replaced. The rear garden area is spacious and the rear entrance once again, just like the Castle de Béthune, has a flight of steps leading to it. On these, no doubt countless photographs of the pilots of the various *jastas* based here at the time were taken (*Jasta*s 1, 11, 12, 33, 34 and 59 all used Roucourt). And like Marckebeke, the reader should note that the château is a <u>private</u> residence.

There is also the well-known photograph of the line up of *Jasta* 11's Albatros DIIIs (page 43 of the Harleyford book). Von Richthofen's all-red

DIII is second from the front as the line-up heads away into the distance. At the end of the line stands a couple of canvas hangars and just behind them, to the left, is a mill with its chimney, which has since been demolished.

Another equally famous photo taken here is the group of pilots by the side of the Baron's red Albatros, with him in the cockpit and brother Lothar sitting cross-legged on the ground in front of them. It was a deadly bunch: Karl Allmenröder, Hans Hintsch, Sebastian Festner, Karl-Emil Schäfer, Kurt Wolff, Georg Simon, Otto Brauneck, Karl Effers and Constantin Krefft.

Jasta 11 fought most of Bloody April from this location, remaining here till 10 June at which time it moved to Harlebeke/Bavichove prior to the formation of *JG* I. (see page 24) Von Richthofen had brought his score to 52 by the end of April 1917 and gone home on leave.

Return on the D135 to the N45 and turn right. Turn right on the D140 to Monchecourt. In Monchecourt turn left at the roundabout to the cemetery which is on the left.

Auberchicourt British Cemetery

Auberchicourt was occupied by the Germans throughout the war, until its capture in October 1918 during the final offensive. The cemetery was begun that month, and used until February 1919 during which time the 6th, 23rd and 1st Canadian Casualty Clearing Stations were based in the area. After the armistice further burials were brought in from the surrounding areas, so that now the cemetery contains 288 graves, all but nineteen of whom are identified. The brick wall enclosing the cemetery is unusual in that it is not capped with stone.

There are three aircrew graves within the cemetery, and the one we have come to see is that of Robert Farquhar. It is diagonally across the cemetery from the entrance, to the left of the Cross of Sacrifice. There are two half rows to the left of the Cross, and Farquhar's grave is in the nearer of the two rows, and is the second grave from the far end.

Robert Wallace Farquhar (II B 8)

The co-author of this book first published the identity of this victory in his co-authored book *Under the Guns of the Red Baron* (Franks, Giblin & McCreary, Grub Street, 1995).

He established that Lieutenant R W Farquhar, the pilot of a 23 Squadron Spad VII was the 54th victory 'claimed' by Richthofen on 23 June 1917. 'Claimed' in that for a long time this victory caused a

Pilots of 32 Squadron in 1918. Lieutenant R W Farquhar stands second from the right and Captain A Callender is fourth from the left. Both were killed by *Jasta* 2 on 30 October 1918. Farquhar survived an encounter with the Baron on 23 June 1917 although claimed as victory No.54.

considerable amount of head scratching amongst researchers, as no casualty on the day seemed to fit the circumstances of the action.

Eventually it was realised that there was no casualty – Farquhar and his aircraft had survived the action. Only then, with the benefit of hindsight, was it realised that von Richthofen's combat report does not actually state that he saw his victim crash. It concludes:

> *At first the plane began to smoke, then fell, turning and turning to the ground, two kilometres north of Ypres, without having been caught.*

Norman Franks, digging into the records of the only two RFC Spad units in France – 19 and 23 Squadrons – could find no losses either, but then by chance he stumbled on a missing flight record book of 23 Squadron's (or to be more accurate, a few pages in a Wing file), and discovered that at 2015 hours on the on the 23rd, three Spads had encountered nine Albatros Scouts and that in the brief fight that ensued, one of the British machines had been hit in the radiator and petrol tank then spun away.

The Spads were on an offensive patrol to the north of Ypres when they spotted a formation of Albatros scouts. Farquhar was seen to single out an Albatros and attack it, only to be attacked in turn by another. His aircraft was observed to go down, and then because of the general melée of the action, nothing more was seen of it. How Farquhar succeeded in landing is not known, but he must have done so, and although his aircraft was damaged, it must have been repaired within the squadron as no loss report was completed. It is still unclear if

Farquhar got down at his home base or the airfield at Elverdinge.

What von Richthofen had described in his combat report as smoke, was in fact a combination of vaporised petrol and steaming water escaping from the Spad's holed radiator, while the pilot, far from hit himself, was merely spinning down out of the danger area and switching off his engine. In the evening gloom, von Richthofen had claimed his victim down on fire, and 'witnessed' by other German airmen and probably by German troops too, he was able to have his 'victory' confirmed. The Spad, according to von Richthofen, had gone down two kilometres north of Ypres although he did not actually mention it had crashed.

Robert Farquhar was born on 4 February 1898, the son of George and Florence Farquhar of 528 Lordship Lane, Dulwich, London, SE22. Robert joined the Royal Flying Corps in 1916, and his first posting in France was with 18 Squadron, with whom he scored his first victory. He then transferred to 23 Squadron, flying Spads as we have seen, achieving another five victories by July 1917, so becoming an ace in his own right, and during which time he had his encounter with von Richthofen.

Ernst Bormann, *Jasta* 2, who, with Alfred Lindenberger, shot down Callender and Farquhar on 30 October 1918. Bormann, from Holzminden, was a week short of his 21st birthday, ending the war with 16 victories.

By the early summer of 1918 he was instructing at the No. 1 School of Flying and Gunnery before joining 32 Squadron in France, flying the SE5a. He was killed less than two weeks before the end of the war, on the morning of 30 October 1918 on an offensive patrol. He was still only twenty years old.

Go straight ahead to the stop sign and turn right. Continue over the stop signs and junctions. At the traffic lights turn right on to the D943 and continue south east through Bouchain. At a T junction turn left on the N30. Pass over the level crossing and turn right on the D74 to Avesnes-le-Sec. In the village follow the D88 to Haspres. Take the second and last turn to the right into a side street and as the road bends to the right turn left and follow the farm track until just past the last house.

Avesnes-le-Sec German Aerodrome

The airfield here is sometimes referred to as Avesnes, Cambrai, despite the town of Cambrai being some 20 or so kilometres to the south-west. The site of the aerodrome is surrounded by a circle of villages: Iwuy, Haspres, Montrécourt and Villers-en-Cauchies. *Jasta* 11 operated from here from 22 November 1917 through to 19 March 1918, while *Jasta* 4 and *Jasta* 6 flew from Lieu-St-Armand, just to the north, and *Jasta* 10 used an airfield at Iwuy, to the south-west.

Von Richthofen had not added to his score of 61, secured on 3 September 1917, till the day after the move to Avesnes. For the rest of September and into most of October

Baron von Richthofen.

he was on leave but the next offensive saw his return. The Battle of Cambrai opened on 20 November and was to last until 3 December. During that period, victory No.62 came on 23 November near Bourlon Wood, the pilot of the downed DH5 being wounded but safe within his own lines. A week later came No.63, an SE5a, whose pilot, D A D I MacGregor, was never found. Then the Baron went on leave again on 12 December, not returning to the Front until February.

Even then he did not score again until March, though he added three more to his total while still operating from Avesnes. The first of the three was a Bristol Fighter of 62 Squadron, brought down on 12 March. It was a disastrous day for this unit as these were their first operational losses and four machines failed to return. One was claimed by Manfred, two by his brother Lothar and the fourth by *Leutnant* Steinhauser, also of *Jasta* 11. The next two claims by von Richthofen were Sopwith Camels and fortunately both pilots survived as prisoners.

On 19 and 20 March *Jasta*s 6, 10 and 11 of *Jagdgeschwader* I moved base, followed by *Jasta* 4 on the 26th.

SE5 pilot Lieutenant D MacGregor, 41 Squadron, was shot down on 30 November 1917 whilst the Baron flew from Avesnes le Sec. MacGregor has no known grave.

81

Avesnes-le-Sec
German Aerodrome

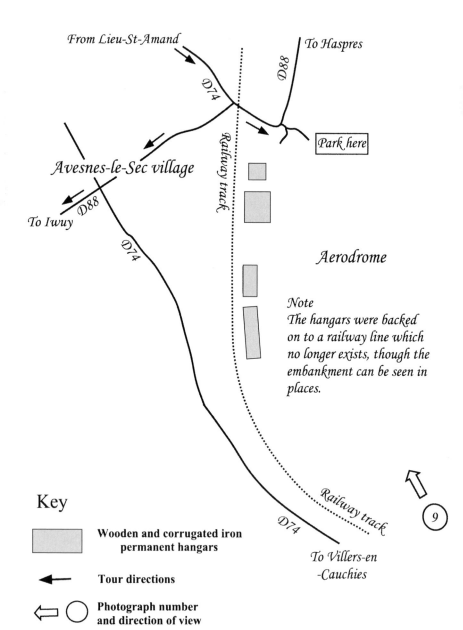

From Lieu-St-Amand

To Haspres

D88

D74

Park here

Avesnes-le-Sec village

Railway track

To Iwuy

D88

D74

Aerodrome

Note
The hangars were backed on to a railway line which no longer exists, though the embankment can be seen in places.

Railway track

D74

9

To Villers-en-Cauchies

Key

Wooden and corrugated iron permanent hangars

Tour directions

Photograph number and direction of view

Photograph No. 9: Avesnes-le-Sec looking north in 2003.

Return to the D88 and go left downhill. At the cross roads continue ahead on the D88 to Iwuy. Pass over a level crossing and at the traffic lights go left. Follow the N30 to Cambrai. At the Cambrai ring road go left to Compiegne and St Quentin. Continue on the ring road until you pick up Arras signs and follow these on to the D939 to Arras. Pass over a railway bridge, turn right onto the one-way system, then left on the ring road. The memorial will appear on the left and you will have to go through the central reservation of the dual carriageway to reach the parking area.

The Air Forces Memorial to the Missing

The Air Force Memorial to the Missing at Faubourg d'Amiens is an imposing memorial with many names to conjure with. Take some time to scan the names, many famous and familiar will be found here. Spot too a new one – Second Lieutenant G W B Bradford, of 15 Squadron. Somehow his name has been missing from any memorial since his death on 4 February 1917, the eleventh victory of the German ace Erwin Böhme. Böhme flew with von Richthofen in *Jasta* 2 under the tutelage of Oswald Boelcke. The lack of any grave or memorial for

Bradford was discovered by Hal Giblin, co-author with Norman Franks of their book *Under the Guns of the Kaiser's Aces* (see Further Reading section) in which they described the victories of four German aces, one of whom was Böhme. Following representation to the Commonwealth War Graves Commission, they finally acknowledged the omission and had his name added to the Addenda panel on the Arras Memorial.

For a list of the names of the missing involved in combats with von Richthofen, please refer to Appendix A. The number is formidable – 45! Among them are many stories of interest but we shall confine ourselves to just a few.

Richard Applin

Applin of 19 Squadron fell to the Baron on 29 April 1917, the first of four victories scored by the German ace on this day, before he left the front for some leave. It seems obvious that von Richthofen was trying to make his total score a nice round 50 before he left; in fact his total reached 52 by the time the day ended.

19 Squadron, based at Vert Galand (see page 149) was only one of two units in the RFC who operated the French Spad VII fighter. The story goes that word came that the Circus was over the front and that 19 Squadron's CO – Major H D Harvey-Kelly DSO (famous for being the first British airman to land his aeroplane in France after war had been declared in 1914) – decided to take a patrol out to do battle. If the story has any truth in it, then Harvey-Kelly, while being an experienced airman was far

Lieutenant R Applin, 19 Squadron, killed 29 April 1917; no known grave.

from being in the front rank of fighter pilots, so it seemed incongruous that he should feel able to engage such a formidable foe with any form of confidence. Added to this his two companions were not over-experienced, so it seems that in all probability Harvey-Kelly was just flying a normal patrol.

In the event *Jasta* 11 engaged the three Spads and shot them all down. H-K and Applin were both killed, with the third pilot, Lieutenant W N Hamilton, luckily being taken prisoner. Just why H-K felt it necessary to fly this morning is another question. At this stage of the war, COs were not encouraged to fly operationally, often being ordered not to do so, for fear of their command experience being lost to the flying corps. H-K had no need to impress anyone, and the fact too that General Hugh Trenchard, in command of the RFC in France, was coming to dine at 19 Squadron's Mess that lunchtime, makes it seem all the more incongruous that he should risk not being on hand to greet the head of the RFC. The great man duly arrived and finally had to leave without seeing Harvey-Kelly, and probably guessed that he would never see him again.

A E Cuzner

On the 29 April 1917 the Baron's fourth kill of the day was an RNAS pilot, Flight Sub-Lieutenant Albert Edward Cuzner from Canada. For many years the identity of who was victory number 52 was obscured by the fact that Floyd Gibbons, writing his book on von Richthofen in the 1920s, doctored Richthofen's combat report so that it would fit his research that it had to be a Nieuport Scout flown by Captain F L Barwell of 40 Squadron. It was the first – and only – Sopwith Triplane von Richthofen shot down and he confused matters by failing to make it clear in his report that it was such. Twenty-seven-year-old Eddy Cuzner was a member of 8 Naval Squadron and on this evening he and several other naval pilots engaged *Jasta* 11 near Douai, and most of them were experienced men. Bob Little, Rex Arnold, Rod McDonald, and Phil Johnston were either aces or would become so. They were also joined by Richard Minifie of 1 Naval in his first major combat, in which he gained his first victories and would go on to score 21 by early 1918. Victor Rowley was another up and coming ace and his report of the action noted the presence of red coloured Albatri. Cuzner's Triplane was set on fire in the air and went down over Henin-Liétard.

Flight Sub-Lieutenant A E Cuzner RNAS, another pilot with no known grave. He was flying a Sopwith Triplane when the Baron shot him down on 29 April 1917, the only Triplane he claimed.

Born on 30 August 1890 he was brought up in Ottawa and attended the University of Toronto and was a fine scholar and sportsman. Cuzner volunteered for the RNAS in May 1916 and took private flying lessons with the Curtiss School in Toronto. Awarded his Royal Aero Club 'ticket', No. 3627, on 3 September 1916, he sailed for England two weeks later. Following further military flying tuition he arrived at Naval 8 on 8 March 1917. he had flown only fifteen patrols before being posted missing on 29 April.

R Raymond-Barker

Lanoe Hawker VC of course is on the Memorial, the fight being mentioned elsewhere in this book. (see page 114) The name above his is another CO, Major Richard Raymond-Barker MC, who commanded 3 Squadron. He was the Baron's 79th kill, falling in flames on 20 April 1918 in the German's final successful air fight.

Born on 6 May 1894 Raymond-Barker was farming in Canada when war broke out. He returned immediately and enlisted as a private in the Middlesex Regiment but received a commission by the end of November 1914. Learning to fly the following summer he transferred to the RFC on 6 August 1915. In November he was posted to 6 Squadron in France and spent the next year at the Front with 16 Squadron as well. In May 1917 he was posted to 48 Squadron as a flight commander and also served in 11 Squadron in the same capacity, flying two-seater Bristol Fighters. He and his observers claimed six enemy machines and in August his Military Cross was

The Raymond-Barker family before the war. Richard is sitting on the ground, with brother Aubrey seated cross-legged on the right. Aubrey was shot down flying with 12 Squadron in October 1916, and taken prisoner.

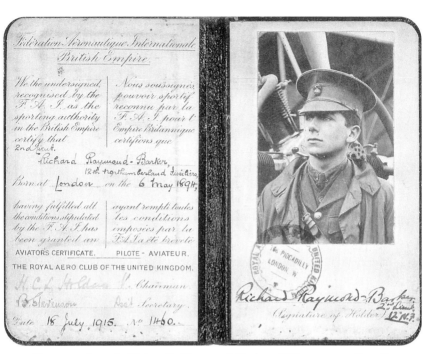

The experienced Major R Raymond-Barker MC, commanding 3 Squadron RAF. Killed in action 20 April 1918, victory No.79.

gazetted. In the same month he was promoted to major and given command of 3 Squadron, who operated the legendary Sopwith Camel.

He was another squadron commander who need not have been flying, but at least had the sense to accompany his men on this patrol rather than lead, leaving that to a flight commander more in tune with up-to-date single-seater fighter tactics. Not that Raymond-Barker was inexperienced, it was just that his experience was of an earlier period of the war and in two-seat fighters rather than a single-seat Camel. Despite the experienced flight commander leading, it would seem the Camel patrol was surprised from behind and that Raymond-Barker had no inkling of danger until bullets began to rip into his machine. Once the flames started, that was the end. His body was never recovered and thus his name is commemorated on the Arras memorial.

Raymond-Barker's younger brother Aubrey was taken prisoner-of-war on 21 October 1916 whilst flying with 12 Squadron. One of the other pilots in the patrol was Second Lieutenant J G Cameron, who became von Richthofen's eighth victim just over two weeks later.

A S Todd

A further naval pilot listed is yet another 8 Naval Squadron Canadian. Flight Lieutenant Allan Switzer Todd, from Georgetown, Ontario, was Richthofen's 16th victory, claimed on 4 January 1917.

Born on 18 April 1886 he was the son of a doctor in Toronto. He joined the RNAS on 6 September 1915, having learned to fly at the Curtiss School in Toronto and received his Royal Aero Club certificate, No. 1725 just two days earlier. After some time at Dover he was posted to 1 Wing in November 1916.

Jasta 11 had seen four aircraft above but as they were not being fired upon by German AA guns, they thought initially they were German. Only when they got closer did they see they were British Sopwith Pups. One came down and attacked von Richthofen, and straight away the Baron realised the Pup was more manoeuvrable than his Albatros DII, but his skill overcame his

Flight Lieutenant A S Todd, 8 Squadron RNAS. Killed in action on 4 January 1917, he became victory No.16, the first for the new year, and brought the Baron the coveted *Pour le Mérite*.

adversary and as the Pup went down it began to fall apart. Todd was 20 years old.

Being his 16th victory, this put von Richthofen firmly in line for the prized *Pour le Mérite* he was eagerly chasing, the score necessary for this award having been raised from eight to sixteen, just before von Richthofen gained his eighth in November 1916. The Blue Max was awarded on 12 January 1917.

G O Smart

Our final casualty is Second Lieutenant George Orme Smart, the Baron's 37th victory, downed on 7 April 1917. This came at the start of the Bloody April period, in which the RFC suffered terrible casualties due to obsolete equipment and having to employ aggressive tactics. The 60 Squadron patrol was, according to the Baron's report, still over

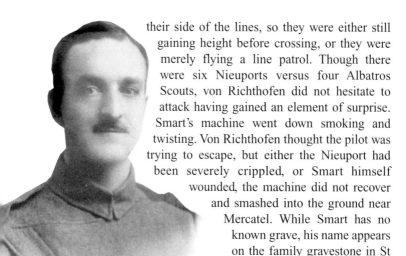

their side of the lines, so they were either still gaining height before crossing, or they were merely flying a line patrol. Though there were six Nieuports versus four Albatros Scouts, von Richthofen did not hesitate to attack having gained an element of surprise. Smart's machine went down smoking and twisting. Von Richthofen thought the pilot was trying to escape, but either the Nieuport had been severely crippled, or Smart himself wounded, the machine did not recover and smashed into the ground near Mercatel. While Smart has no known grave, his name appears on the family gravestone in St Paul's Churchyard, Kersal, Lancashire, close to where the 31-year old had lived.

Smart, born on 17 August 1886, was educated privately and at Shrewsbury School. After leaving school he joined the family firm of cotton manufacturers in Manchester. He enlisted in the RFC in August 1916 and in October gained his Royal Aero Club certificate, No. 3707.

Second Lieutenant G O Smart of 60 Squadron has no known grave, although his death on 7 April 1917 is commemorated on the family plot in St Paul's Churchyard, Kersal, Lancashire.

Following flying training with 56 Squadron (later to be famous when Albert Ball and Jimmy McCudden served in it) he arrived at 60 Squadron in France as a sergeant pilot on 17 January 1917. Just over a month later, on 21 February, he was promoted to second lieutenant on probation but was confirmed in his rank the same day. Just six weeks later he was killed in action.

Return to the centre of Arras. This concludes the second tour.

The Southern Area

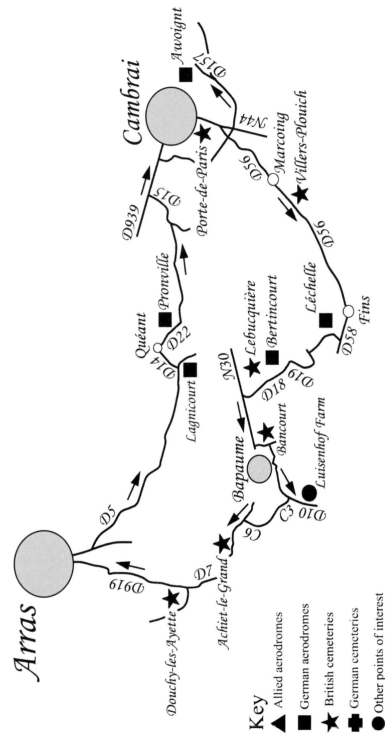

Arras

Cambrai

Douchy-les-Ayette
D919
D7
Achiet-le-Grand
C6
Bapaume
C3
Bancourt
D10
Luisenhof Farm
N30
D18
D19
Lebucquière
Bertincourt
Léchelle
Fins
D58
D56
Villers-Plouich
Marcoing
D56
N44
D157
Awoingt
Porte-de-Paris
D939
D15
Pronville
Quéant
D22
D14
Lagnicourt
D5

Key

▲ Allied aerodromes
■ German aerodromes
★ British cemeteries
✚ German cemeteries
● Other points of interest
← Tour directions

Chapter Three

THE SOUTHERN AREA

The third part of our tour looks at places which were mainly associated with the early days of von Richthofen's career as a fighter pilot.

Lagnicourt German Aerodrome – *Jasta Boelcke*
Pronville German Aerodrome – Last days in *Jasta 2*
Awoingt German Aerodrome – March 1918
Porte-de-Paris Cemetery – L B F Morris 11 Squadron
Villers-Plouich Communal Cemetery – T Rees 11 Squadron
Léchelle British Aerodrome – *JG* I March/April 1918
Bertincourt German Aerodrome – First victory
Lebucquière Communal Cemetery Extension – 19 Squadron
Bancourt Communal Cemetery – 11 and 21 Squadrons
Luisenhof Farm – Lanoe Hawker VC 24 Squadron
Achiet-le-Grand Communal Cemetery Extension – G Doughty
Douchy-les-Ayette British Cemetery – A G Knight 29 Squadron

Leave Arras on the Bapaume road, then turn left on the D5 to Neuville-Vitasse. Follow the D5 through Lagnicourt village. Just after the leaving village sign there is a line of electricity pylons. Stop under these and the aerodrome is on the right.

Lagnicourt German Aerodrome

The airfield site is where von Richthofen, Boelcke and the rest of *Jasta* 2 moved to on 22 September 1916, having been forced to evacuate Bertincourt by Allied shelling. (see page 108) It remained here till 4 December, and operating from this base *Jasta* 2 had its most successful time. Over 60 Allied aircraft were claimed destroyed, but these successes were tinged with sadness for the pilots of the new *staffel*. On 28 October 1916 the great Boelcke collided with Erwin Böhme's Albatros during a battle with DH2s of 24 Squadron RFC, falling to his death, while on 22 November, his successor, Stefan Kirmaier was shot down and killed by pilots of 24 Squadron.

Lagnicourt Aerodrome

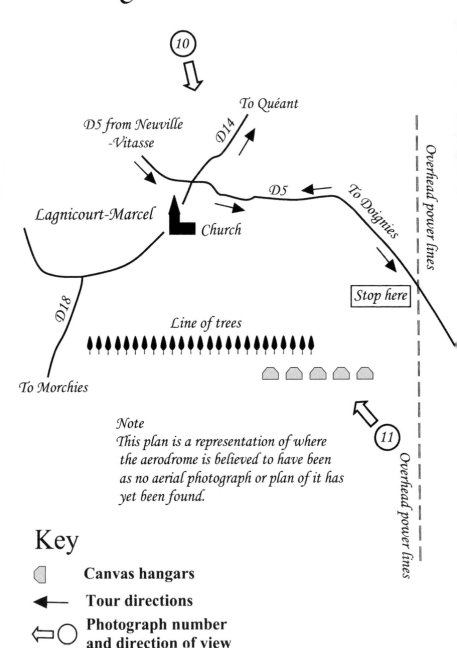

To Quéant

D5 from Neuville
-Vitasse

D14

Lagnicourt-Marcel

Church

D5

To Doignies

Overhead power lines

Stop here

D18

Line of trees

To Morchies

Note
This plan is a representation of where
the aerodrome is believed to have been
as no aerial photograph or plan of it has
yet been found.

Overhead power lines

Key

Canvas hangars

Tour directions

Photograph number
and direction of view

Photograph No. 10: Lagnicourt looking south in 2004.

At Boelcke's funeral, held in the Cathedral at Cambrai on 31 October, Manfred von Richthofen carried the Boelcke's *Ordenskissen*. This was a black cushion on which was pinned the dead man's orders, decorations and awards. After the ceremony the coffin was taken to Boelcke's home town for burial.

While at Lagnicourt, von Richthofen gained ten victories, bringing his score to eleven, not the least of which the last was the man the German's called, the 'English Boelcke' – Lanoe Hawker VC. (see page 114)

Photograph No. 11: Oswald Boelcke, the Baron's mentor, in his Albatros DII at Lagnicourt in the autumn of 1916. His successor, Stefan Kirmaier is second from the left while *Leutnant* Erich König has the white hat band. Manfred stands far left.

Return to the centre of the village and turn right on the D14 to Quéant and go right on the D14 to Pronville. Then continue on the D22 to Pronville. Continue through the village on the D22 towards Inchy-en-Artois. Pass the first set of white posts on the left side of the road to a farm track on the right and park. Ahead can be seen another set of white posts. The aerodrome was probably between these two sets of posts on the left.

Pronville German Aerodrome

The close spelling of Proville and Pronville has led over the years to confusion between these two locations.

Jasta 2 were at Pronville after leaving Lagnicourt on 5 December 1916. Proville is on the western outskirts of Cambrai, while Pronville is some kilometres west from Cambrai, north of the N30. It is only a short distance from Lagnicourt and just to the south-east of Quéant. By the time *Jasta* 2 moved to Proville, via Eswars on 23 March 1917, the Baron had left. During his time at Pronville he claimed five British machines, victories twelve to sixteen and on 12 January received the coveted *Pour le Mérite*. Two days later he left to command *Jasta* 11.

So it was at Pronville that von Richthofen served out his last days with this famous *jasta*, it having been named *Jasta Boelcke*, by Royal Decree from November 1916 in memory of its first illustrious leader. *Jasta* 11 was the only *jagdstaffel* to score more victories in the First World War than *Jasta Boelcke,* 350 as opposed to 336. Von Richthofen instilled in his *Jasta* 11 pilots the same aggressive hunting techniques

Pronville looking west in April 2004.

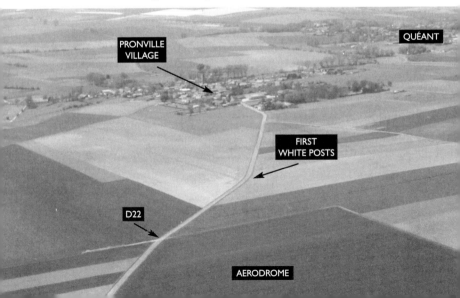

and skills he himself had been taught by the master – Oswald Boelcke.

The area around here with villages like Quéant, Bullecourt and Croisilles, are all names featured in combat reports of the time as this was a much fought over area. It was from Pronville that von Richthofen unknowingly fought one of the RFC's future aces some way off to the west. We are not looking for a location this time, merely an area of sky above Ficheux to the southwest of Arras. It is in this piece of airspace that von Richthofen fought three DH2s of 29 Squadron and claimed one as his 15th victory on 27 December 1916. The identity of the machine and indeed the pilot took many years to sort out, due mainly to the fact that von Richthofen did not actually succeed in shooting down his opponent. In fact none of the 300 rounds he fired at the DH2 even hit it! It was also recorded incorrectly as a larger FE2b which did not help historians and researchers.

Lieutenant L G D'Arcy, 18 Squadron, killed in action 20 December 1916 – no known grave.

Richthofen versus McCudden

Returning to his base at Pronville, von Richthofen claimed a *gitterrumpf* shot down into the British lines above Ficheux. The Germans called all pusher-types, ie: those machines with the engine behind the pilot's gondola, the tail being fitted at the end of two sets of strutted booms, as *gitterrumpfs* – literally 'lattice-tailed' – and a *gitterrumpf* was duly acknowledged as the Baron's 15th kill.

nacelle

He had no reason to think his shots had totally missed hitting the British 'pusher' machine, especially as it had fallen in a spinning nose dive for more than 9,000 feet and when he last saw it, it was close to the ground, *so must have crashed*. When asked, front line observers confirmed seeing this *gitterrumpf* fall as indicated, so it was confirmed as having (obviously) crashed. When historians later tried to identify this victory, the nearest anyone could get was a pusher FE2b of 11 Squadron which had been a casualty that day, so the Baron's *gitterrumpf* became this 'lattice-tailed' FE. The fact that the location and the time did not match up was an unsolved discrepancy. Having dug deeper, we now know that the machine was a DH2 and its pilot was none other than the soon to be famous James McCudden MM, in December 1916 still a lowly NCO sergeant-pilot (later Major

Sergeant J T B McCudden MM, claimed by the Baron as his 15th victory, in reality his DH2 fighter was not even hit. He is receiving his French *Croix de Guerre* from General Joffre at Lillers in January 1916.

McCudden VC DSO* MC* MM CdG). McCudden in his book *Flying Fury* fully describes his fight on the 27th which matches von Richthofen's action exactly.

As the Baron was eagerly chasing his *Pour le Mérite* at this juncture, he allowed his mind's eye to 'see' the 'pusher' crash rather than admit it might have had time to pull out of its spin and fly off, as indeed McCudden had done. It was a close thing nevertheless, and when he did land back at his airfield, his comrades in the fight had already landed and reported him shot down! (For more details of McCudden's life see page 153)

Continue ahead through Inchy-en-Artois and follow the D22 to Sains-les-Marquion then go left on the D15 to Sains-le-Marquion. Stay on the D15 until you go right on the D939 to Cambrai. At a roundabout go right to Cambrai. Follow Cambrai signs over a canal onto the ring road. Leave the ring road right towards Bohain, then go left on the D157 to Awoingt. After the entering village sign at a sharp right turn marked by blue and white chevrons turn left off the road and park. The German aerodrome was backed on to the village which is on your right.

Awoingt German Aerodrome

*Jasta*s 6, 10 and 11 all used this airfield for a few days in March 1918 (*Jasta* 4 was at Lieu-St-Armand, then Léchelle), having transferred from the aerodrome at Avesnes-le-Sec (see page 82) Von Richthofen scoring his 67th and 68th victories while based here. These were an SE5a of 41 Squadron and a Camel of 3 Squadron. Both pilots, Second Lieutenant D Cameron and Lieutenant J P McCone, were killed and have no known grave, being commemorated at Arras. The German March offensive began on the 21 March 1918 and *JG* I had been brought forward the previous day as reinforcements.

Lieutenant J P McCone, 41 Squadron (right). This Canadian died in combat on 24 March 1918 and has no known grave.

Awoingt
German Aerodrome

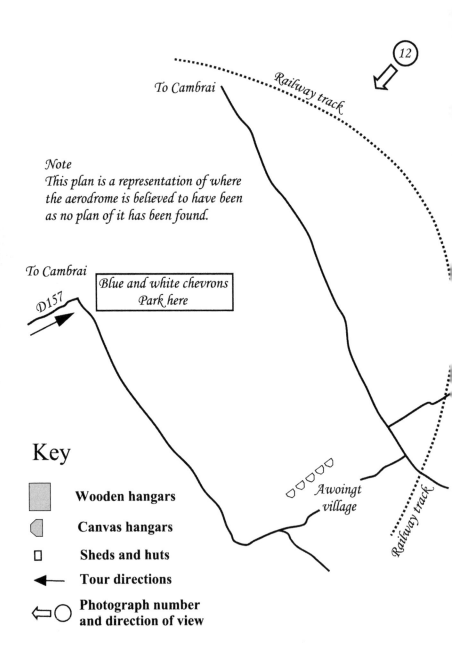

To Cambrai

Railway track

12

Note
This plan is a representation of where
the aerodrome is believed to have been
as no plan of it has been found.

To Cambrai

D157

Blue and white chevrons
Park here

Awoingt
village

Railway track

Key

Wooden hangars

Canvas hangars

Sheds and huts

Tour directions

Photograph number
and direction of view

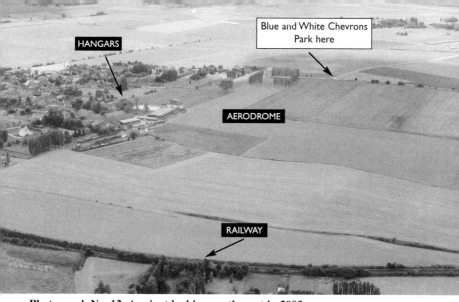

HANGARS

Blue and White Chevrons
Park here

AERODROME

RAILWAY

Photograph No. 12: Awoingt looking south-west in 2003.

As always over an active battle area, von Richthofen was flying his all-red Triplane, not the one partly painted red. He used the all-red one on these occasions for two reasons. Firstly so that his pilots could quickly spot him if they needed to reform, and secondly, so that ground observers could easily identify his machine if he had been involved in a successful combat. A fluid battle area was no place to inspect wrecks of aircraft shot down, so he relied more on air and ground observers to have his claims confirmed.

After only a few days at Awoingt, such was the rapidity of the German advance, *JG* I was moved forward and concentrated on the old British aerodrome at Léchelle. (see page 104)

Return to the Cambrai ring road and turn left. Follow the ring road until you turn left for St Quentin then take the first right signposted Cimetière Militaire. Park outside the cemetery and walk towards the French flag where the British plot can be found.

Second Lieutenant D Cameron was only 18 when shot down by the Baron on 25 March 1918, flying a Camel of 3 Squadron.

Porte-de-Paris Cemetery

The town of Cambrai itself was taken by German troops on 26 August 1914 and despite the British offensive in late 1917, the Battle of Cambrai, was not to be liberated until 8 October 1918. It was heavily mined by the Germans before their withdrawal, and was in a largely ruined condition at the end of the war.

Porte-de-Paris was the more modern of the two Cambrai cemeteries at the time, and was used by the Germans for burials throughout the war. At one time it contained the graves of German, French, Russian, Rumanian and Belgian, as well as British dead. After the war some rationalisation of the graves was carried out, the German ones being removed, and the British being rearranged into two plots, either side of the local war memorial in the centre of the cemetery. As one of the occasional incongruities of CWGC graveyards, there is a single grave of a New Zealand officer, originally buried in St. Olle, by itself on the north side of the cemetery.

The British plot is near the French, and the easiest way to find the right part of the cemetery is to look for the French *Tricolor* and head towards it. There are seven airmen buried here.

One is Flight Sub-Lieutenant W H Hope, who was the first casualty suffered by 8 Naval Squadron, on 24 November 1916. He was shot down by Franz Ray of *Jasta* 1 over Moeuvres on the 23rd, dying of his wounds the next day and was buried by the Germans. Two are victims of von Richthofen. The grave of Lionel Morris is in Plot I, while that of Gilbert Hall is in Plot II.

Lionel Bertram Frank Morris (I A 16)

Second Lieutenant L B F Morris has, perhaps, a certain claim to fame, being the pilot of the first aircraft to be shot down by von Richthofen on the morning of 17 September 1916.

On that day, 3 Brigade RFC had decided to mount a bombing raid on Marcoing railway station to the south of Cambrai. The operation was to be carried out by four BE2ds of 12 Squadron, from Avesnes-le-Comte, being flown without observers because of the weight of their bomb loads, escorted by six FE2bs of 11 Squadron, operating from Le Hameau.

Over the target they met Boelcke's

Victim of von Richthofen's first successful combat was Second Lieutenant L B F Morris of 11 Squadron. The Baron shot down his FE2b on 17 September 1916.

Jasta 2, operating as a unit for the first time. A large fight developed, during which the attacking force lost four FEs and two BEs. Two of the bombing aircraft were victims of ground fire, with three FEs being shot down by *Jasta* 2, and one by *Jasta* 4, which had also engaged the British formation.

Von Richthofen attacked the FE of Morris, and his observer Tom Rees, (see page 103) and after several bursts the engine stopped and the aircraft glided down. Rees returned fire throughout the descent, and von Richthofen continued firing until he had killed Rees, shortly before the aircraft reached the ground.

By this stage Morris had also been seriously wounded, but even so he managed to land the FE on the German airfield at Flesquières, to the south west of Cambrai. Von Richthofen landed alongside the British aircraft, and watched as the dead observer and the wounded pilot were removed from their aircraft.

Morris was so seriously wounded that he died before the ambulance could reach the nearby German Military Hospital, but the distance travelled while he was alive was enough to ensure that he was buried in a different cemetery from his observer.

Bertram Morris was born in 1897, and lived with his parents at 'Merle Bank', Rotherfield Road, Carshalton, Surrey, where his father owned a tobacconist's shop. On 13 May 1915, just after his eighteenth birthday, he was selected for induction into the Inns of Court OTC, and he was commissioned into the West Surreys, the Queen's Royal Regiment, on 20 August 1915.

He immediately applied for a transfer to the Royal Flying Corps, and gained his Royal Aero Club Aviators Certificate, No. 2334, on 25 January 1916. In April 1916 he was appointed flying officer, and proceeded to France shortly afterwards.

By coincidence, lying in Porte-de-Paris Cemetery, he and his observer Tom Rees are almost equidistant from Marcoing, their target on 17 September.

Gilbert Sudbury Hall (II A 1)

20 November 1916 was a significant occasion for von Richthofen, as it was the first time he claimed two aircraft in one day.

His first claim was made after a patrol in the morning with *Jasta* 2, with both von Richthofen and *Oberleutnant* Stefan Kirmaier claiming an aircraft shot down. The two British aircraft were brought down within a few minutes and a few kilometres of each other.

Research has failed to find evidence of two allied losses for the correct time and location, and it now seems that von Richthofen and

Kirmaier may have independently claimed what was, in fact, the same aircraft. This was a BE2c of 15 Squadron which had taken off at 0650 hours from Clairfaye Farm, Lealvillers to the north west of Albert, on an artillery observation patrol. Just under two hours later it was seen being driven down by a hostile aircraft seemingly under control, and an hour later a British aircraft was seen upside down in the same area behind German lines. Its crew of Second Lieutenant J C Lees and Lieutenant T H Clarke were taken prisoner and survived the war.

The second victory is much more certain. It was an FE2b of 18 Squadron shot down near Grandcourt at 1515 hours. Although the squadron records are quite sketchy, it is known that the aircraft, crewed by Second Lieutenants G S Hall and G Doughty, had taken off two hours earlier

Second Lieutenant G S Hall, 18 Squadron, wounded in action 20 November 1916, he died ten days later, and is another to lie outside the walls of Cambrai.

from Lavieville on a front line defensive patrol along the 5th Army front. Von Richtohofen in his combat report gives details of the crew names and the correct location. George Doughty the observer was killed at once and is buried in Achiet-le-Grand Cemetery. (see page 115)

Gilbert Hall the pilot was taken to Cambrai Hospital and died ten days later, on the 30th, hence his burial some distance from his observer. He was born on 28 December 1890 and lived with his parents at 'Greenaleigh', Matlock, Derbyshire. He attended Mill Hill School in London, then Burton Bank College where he qualified as an engineer.

Commissioned into the RFC on 13 December 1915, he gained his Royal Aero Club Aviators Certificate, No. 2286, on 16 January 1916. Shortly after arriving in France he was wounded, and although the injury was not serious, it was a 'Blighty', so that he returned to England to recover. He returned to the Front and 18 Squadron on 7 November 1916, just under a fortnight before he was shot down.

Follow the one way system back to the N44 then go right. At a roundabout turn right on the D56 to Marcoing then almost immediately left on the D56 to Marcoing. Turn right on the D15 towards Villers-Plouich and pass over the bridge in to Marcoing. At a roundabout take the left D256 to Villers-Plouich then on to the D56 out of the village. The cemetery is on the left approaching the village of Villers-Plouich.

Villers-Plouich Communal Cemetery

Villers-Plouich was captured by the 13/East Surreys in April 1917 when the Germans retreated to the Hindenburg Line, and was in the British front line during the Battle of Cambrai in November. Lost in March 1918 during the German spring offensive, operation 'Michael', it was regained at the end of September during the final advance, when the 1/East Surreys were the first troops to re-enter the village. After the war it was adopted by the Borough of Wandsworth.

There are over fifty graves here, some unidentified, but only one airman, Tom Rees, the observer of Lionel Morris, the other member of the first crew to be shot down by von Richthofen, as mentioned in the Porte de Paris entry above. His grave is one of two isolated graves at the right hand end of the main part of the civilian cemetery.

Tom Rees (C 2)

Tom Rees lived with his parents, Thomas and Alice Rees, at 'Troed y rhiw Villa', Devynock, Brecon. He had entered Aberystwyth University in 1913, and being an enthusiastic member of the OTC, wished to join up as soon as war was declared in 1914.

He was prevailed upon to wait until he had completed his degree, but as soon as he had been awarded his Batchelor of Arts he applied for the army, and was commissioned into the 14th (Service) Battalion, the Royal Welsh Fusiliers on 21 January 1915, a Pals battalion recruiting from the coastal areas of North Wales, largely the counties of Caernarvon and Anglesey.

His abilities ensured that he was rapidly promoted to lieutenant, and soon after arriving in France in November 1915 he requested a transfer to the Royal Flying Corps. He returned to England to complete his training, and then joined 11 Squadron as an observer. Dead when he was removed from his aircraft, Rees was buried with full military honours by the members of *Jasta* 4.

It was perhaps ironic that Rees had

Although shot down with his pilot Lionel Morris on 17 September 1916, Tom Rees was buried in Villers-Plouich cemetery.

103

been promoted to captain on the day of his death. Even more ironic was the fact that on the same day, 17 September 1917, Rees's brother John was also killed, when he was struck by lightning.

Continue through the village on the D56 to Gouzeaucourt and then go ahead on the D917. In Fins turn right on the D58 to Equancourt. At the cross road proceed ahead on the D172 to Mesnil. At the first cross road turn right down a side road to the farm marked by a large concrete tower visible from the main road. Park by the tower.

Léchelle British Aerodrome

As the rapid German advance of March 1918 continued von Richthofen and his men had to move forward to stay in contact with their army.

Léchelle had earlier been an RFC aerodrome, No. 3 Squadron having been based here from August to October 1917, and 15 Squadron in October and November 1917, and again from early December 1917 till March 1918, when it had to retreat because of the German offensive. Unfortunately for the RAF, but happily for *JG* I, the British did not make a good job of destroying things of use to the enemy, so von Richthofen and his men were quickly able to repair and

Photograph No. 13: Léchelle or Quatre Vent Farm looking south-east in 1999.

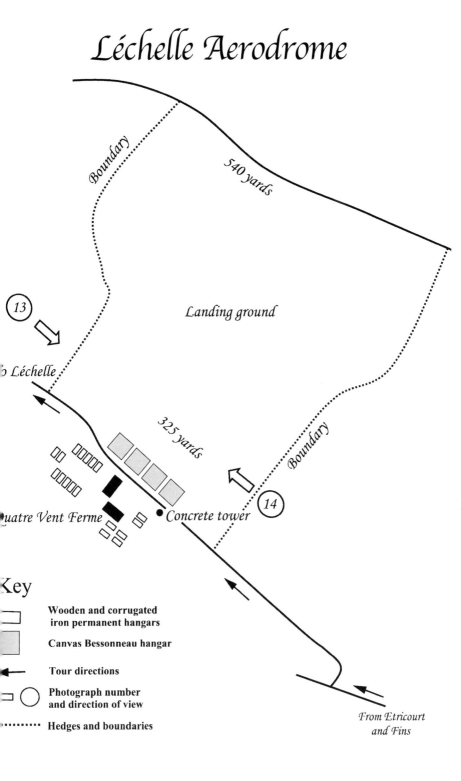

Léchelle Aerodrome

Boundary

540 yards

Landing ground

⑬

o Léchelle

325 yards

Boundary

⑭

uatre Vent Ferme

Concrete tower

Key

Wooden and corrugated
iron permanent hangars

Canvas Bessonneau hangar

Tour directions

Photograph number
and direction of view

Hedges and boundaries

From Etricourt
and Fins

Photograph No. 14: *Jagdesgeschwade*r I at Léchelle with the repaired British Bessonneau hangars on the left.

82 Squadron flew the AWFK8 'Big Ack' similar to the one here, for bombing and close support work.

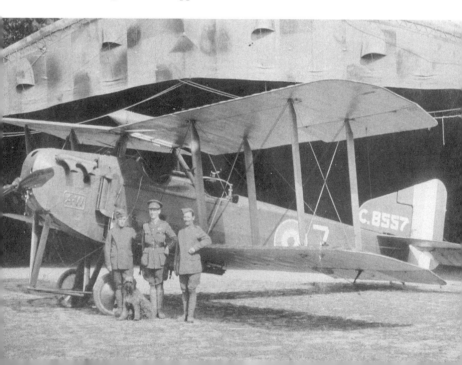

use four Bessonneau aircraft hangars and all of the Armstrong and Nissen huts were left virtually intact. These were a vast improvement on their usual accommodation of tents.

Jagdgeschwader Nr. I operated from here from 26 March to 11 April 1918, although *Jasta*s 6 and 10 moved out on the 3rd, and *Jasta* 4 moved out a day earlier and flew from Harbonnières. There is a famous picture of von Richthofen's quarters at Léchelle with his dog Moritz sitting on a sandbag protecting-wall outside. What appears to be a covered slit trench is in the foreground, no doubt available if British bombers paid the airfield a visit.

Von Richthofen claimed ten victories while *JG* 1 was based here and in fact he was only to bring down two more victims before being killed.

With the see-saw nature of advance and retreat on this part of the front the RAF reoccupied the airfield in October 1918.

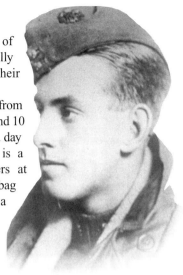

Second Lieutenant J B Taylor, 82 Squadron. He and his observer were killed in action on 28 March 1918, and neither have known graves. Taylor was 19 years old, Second Lieutenant E Betley, 21.

Continue ahead in to Léchelle. At the T junction turn left and proceed over the motorway in to Bus on the D19E. Then go ahead on the D19 to Bertincourt. Go left on the D7 to Bapaume and then the D18 to Vélu. Park just before you reach the large wood ahead on the right.

Richthofen's quarters at Léchelle, with Moritz lying on sandbags right of centre.

Bertincourt German Aerodrome

South of Lebucquiére are the sites of two airfields, Vélu and Bertincourt. Bertincourt is where *Jasta 2* was formed in August 1916 by Oswald Boelcke, and where von Richthofen soon arrived as a founder pilot. By the summer of 1916 Bertincourt was already a famous German airfield, Fokker *Eindeckers* of *KEK* Bertincourt (*Kampfeinsitzer Kommando*, also known as *Einsitzerstaffel* Bertincourt), had operated from here since the start of the year. This unit was later known as *AKN – Abwehr Kommando Nord*. Just to the north is Vélu (on the D18) which was in reality the other side of the airfield, and this is where *Jasta 2* had its first buildings shortly after its formation.

Until late summer 1916 the *Eindeckers* had operated in small numbers attached to two-seater units. With the introduction of machines like the DH2 and FE2 aerial supremacy swung in favour of the British. The Germans realised that dedicated fighter units were needed and the result was the formation of the first *jastas*. Boelcke had a reasonably free hand in selecting his pilots and one of those he chose was Manfred von Richthofen, who he had met during a visit to the Eastern Front. Von Richthofen was not to disappoint his mentor. It was while based here that Manfred claimed the first of an eventual total of 80 victories, making him the most successful fighter pilot of any side in the First World War. His first victim was an FE2 of 11 Squadron and

Photograph No. 15: Bertincourt or Vélu aerodrome in 2004 looking south-east.

the two occupants, Second Lieutenant L B F Morris and his observer Lieutenant T Rees, died. (see page 100)

With the gradual advance of the British during the Battle of the Somme Bertincourt gradually came in range of artillery fire. On 21 September 1916 *Jasta* 2 moved to an aerodrome a few kilometres further back at Lagnicourt. (see page 92)

Continue ahead into Vélu, then go left on the D18 to Lebucquière. In the village go right then right again following the green CWGC signs. The military cemetery is behind the civilian plot.

Lebucquière Communal Cemetery Extension

Lebucquière was in German hands until their retreat to the Hindenburg Line, and was occupied by Allied forces on 19 March 1917. It was recaptured by the Germans almost exactly a year later during the March Offensive of 1918, despite fierce resistance from the 19th (Western) Division. They occupied it for a further six months before it was finally reoccupied by the 5th Division on 3 September 1918 during the final advance.

The extension was begun on 24 March 1917 and was used by the 1st Australian Division and others for the length of the Allied occupation. It was used again in September in the immediate aftermath of the area's recapture.

At the end of the war it contained 150 burials, but was greatly enlarged after the armistice so that now 774 men lie here from the First World War, of whom 266 are unidentified.

Eleven graves contain RFC men, the particular grave we have come to visit being that of John Thompson, located in the near right corner.

John Thompson (III B 27)

Second Lieutenant Thompson, was brought down by the Baron on 16 October 1916 – his fifth victory. He was the pilot of a BE12, one of eight who had taken off from their base at Fienvillers to attack the railway station at Hermies. The BE12 was basically a single-seat fighter version of the ubiquitous two-seater BE2. One of the eight had to drop out with engine problems, but the other seven continued to their target when they were attacked to the west of Havrincourt Wood by five members of *Jasta* 2, including von Richthofen who was flying an Albatros DII.

Thompson was seen going to the aid of another BE12 which was being attacked by three enemy fighters, but was then not seen again.

John Thompson was 23 years old, and was originally from West Bromwich in the Midlands, but by 1914 was living with his widowed mother at 28b North End Road, Hampstead, London.

He volunteered as soon as war broke out, and joined the Honourable Artillery Company (Infantry) on 24 August 1914. After training he joined the 1st Battalion in France on 26 December and stayed with them until he was wounded near Hooge on 16 June 1915 during fighting following the Second Battle of Ypres. Evacuated to England two days later, he was Mentioned in Despatches, and later awarded the Distinguished Conduct Medal. The citation, which appeared in the *London Gazette* on 11 March 1916 stated:

> *1412 Lance Corporal J Thompson, HAC, TF. For conspicuous gallantry. Although wounded, he advanced with his platoon to the first line of a threatened flank and refused to leave his men till he had led them back at the end of the day.*

Second Lieutenant J Thompson DCM, 19 Squadron, buried in Lebucquière Cemetery following his death on 16 October 1916.

Following recovery from his wounds, Thompson was awarded his Royal Aero Club Aviator's Certificate, No. 3082, on 23 May 1916 and was commissioned into the Royal Flying Corps.

Thompson had been with 19 Squadron for only a few days and may even have been on his first operational flight. This, indirectly, was to cause some confusion for later researchers, as von Richthofen stated that the pilot's name was Capper.

There was a pilot of that name with 19 Squadron at the time, Lieutenant Edward Capper, but he was not flying on 16 October, and indeed would survive for another six months before being shot down by Kurt Wolff of *Jasta* 11 on 14 April 1917. Presumably Thompson, being new to the squadron, must have borrowed some item of Capper's with his name on it, and when the wreckage was inspected by German troops they naturally assumed that this was the identity of the pilot.

Return to the D18 and go right then left on the N30 A1 to Paris. In Fremicourt just before the leaving village sign turn left down an unmarked road to Bancourt. Follow the D7E2 to Bapaume and then left on the D7 to Villers-au-Flos. Turn left at the green CWGC sign down to the military cemetery visible across a field. All the graves in which we are interested are on the right in the civilian plot.

Bancourt Communal Cemetery

Bancourt, like all the villages in this area, was in Allied hands for a year until lost in March 1918. It was finally taken by the New Zealand Division, in particular the 2nd Auckland Battalion on 30 August 1918.

The civilian cemetery seems to have been partly cleared leaving isolated headstones. Two of the graves (Clarkson and Lansdale) are right by the gate and the third (Fisher) is to the right. There are only eight military graves here, six of them being aviators, one of whom is unknown. The other two are a New Zealander and an Australian whose grave was subsequently destroyed by shell fire. Of the six fliers, three are victims of von Richthofen.

Ernest Conway Lansdale (2) and Albert Clarkson (3)

Lieutenant E C Lansdale and Sergeant A Clarkson were the crew of an 11 Squadron FE2b which fell to von Richthofen on 30 September 1916, his 3rd victory. Their aircraft was a presentation machine purchased with money raised by the people of Malaya, and bearing the legend 'Malaya No. 22' on its nacelle. It was part of the escort for a bombing raid by aircraft of 12 and 13 Squadrons against *Jasta* 2's own airfield at Lagnicourt. (see page 92).

Whether von Richthofen and his colleagues in *Jasta* 2 were already airborne, or whether they managed to take off and attack the allied formation is not known, but he caught up with the FE at 13,000 feet over the airfield and shot it down. It descended in uncontrolled circles towards the ground and burnt out near Fremicourt.

Lieutenant E C Lansdale, 11 Squadron, became von Richthofen's 3rd victory on 30 September 1916.

Ernest Lansdale, 21, was originally from Goole, but was living with his family at 3 Hawthorn Villas, Grove Road, Ilkley, Yorkshire, when war broke out.

111

Educated at Ilkley Grammar School, he had then joined Leigh and Pierce Limited, Wholesale Provision Merchants. His position as a representative meant that he travelled extensively, and in August 1914 he was on business in Denmark. He returned to England and immediately joined up.

With his education and background, it is perhaps not surprising that he was given a commission in the Army Service Corps on 16 October 1914 and posted to 57th Divisional Train, where his father, Major M E Lansdale, was second in command.

Ernest was promoted to lieutenant on 12 June 1915, and went to France for the first time in the following January. In July 1916 he transferred to the Royal Flying Corps, and after flying training in England joined 11 Squadron on 17 September, just two weeks before his death, and the day von Richthofen gained his first confirmed victory.

Sergeant A Clarkson, Lansdale's observer on 30 September 1916, buried with his pilot.

Sergeant Clarkson, born and brought up at Lonsdale Road, Burnley, Lancashire, was a year older than his pilot. After leaving school he completed his apprenticeship as an electrician with a local company.

He joined the Royal Flying Corps in January 1915, and after completing his observer's training was posted to France. He was an experienced observer and after his death was reported as *having accounted for three German aeroplanes.*

Clarkson's parents had moved to Blackpool in August 1915, and it was there that his father died in early October 1916. In a terrible coincidence, the news of Albert's loss was received by his mother as her husband's entourage was about to leave for the cemetery in their original home town of Burnley.

Arthur James Fisher (9)

Second Lieutenant Fisher was flying a BE12 with 21 Squadron when he fell to von Richthofen on 25 October 1916, as his sixth victory. His was one of five BE12s which had taken off at 0745 hours on an offensive patrol over the lines.

We have met the BE12 before, a version of the BE2 flown as a single-seater aircraft. It was in reality, no fighter, firstly because of its lack of performance, and secondly because the great stability of the aircraft, which was a great asset when being used for photography or artillery spotting, made it difficult to manoeuvre quickly in a dog fight.

Von Richthofen reported that he was alone in his Albatros DII when he attacked the BE12 which crashed to the south of Bapaume. It landed on the German side of the lines, but sufficiently near to the front lines that the wreckage was subjected to heavy fire.

As it was on its way down, other German machines appeared and one attacked the BE12 again. As a result, two pilots claimed him, von Richthofen and *Vizefeldwebel* Hans Karl Müller of *Jasta* 5 (himself already credited with seven victories at the time). But as the German system did not allow for the sharing of victories, arbitration followed and von Richthofen was given the credit.

Arthur Fisher was 21 years old, the son of the Superintendent and Matron of the Clapham branch of Dr. Barnado's Homes, Clapham High Street, London. Amongst the very first to volunteer he joined the 23/(County of London) Battalion, The London Regiment in September 1914. The London Regiment was unique in that all its battalions were territorials, there being no regular army element.

Selected for officer training, he was posted to the Inns of Court Officer Training Corps on 23 October 1915 and, gazetted as a temporary second lieutenant on the General List, he was attached to the Royal Flying Corps for pilot training.

He was awarded his wings, then posted to France in September 1916, arriving at 21 Squadron on 9 October, being shot down just over a fortnight later. Mortally wounded by a bullet in his bowels, he died on 25 October.

After the war, Arthur Fisher's mother was widowed, and subsequently moved to 76 Victoria Road in Clapham. She named the house 'Bancourt' after the cemetery where her son was buried.

Return to the D7 and turn right, cross over the motorway. At a T junction turn right then go left on the D10 to Ligny-Thilloy. Continue through the village on the D10, past the civilian cemetery on the left to the lowest point in the road, marked by a metal crash barrier on the right hand side of the road. The site of Luisenhof Farm is directly opposite on the left side and was 250 yards in to the field.

Luisenhof Farm

By November 1916 Luisenhof Farm was no more than a shell-scarred landscape and the farm buildings just shattered ruins. However, it was here, some 250 yards east of the farm, that Major Lanoe Hawker VC DSO, commander of 24 Squadron, fell and crashed after being hit in the head by a single bullet fired from von Richthofen's Albatros DII.

Hawker was among the first RFC 'heroes' of the First World War. Still a month short of his 26th birthday, he had gained much service experience and in early bombing raids and air combats had earned both the Victoria Cross and Distinguished Service Order.

A pre-war Royal Engineer officer, Hawker had learnt to fly in 1913 and once the war had started saw considerable action with No.6 Squadron RFC. After a rest, he was given command of 24 Squadron, equipped with the new DH2 pusher single-seat fighter, and led this unit to France in February 1916.

At this time there were restrictions against commanding officers flying on operations, being seen as too valuable to the expansion of the RFC to lose, so he rarely led his men in the air. Indeed, one can assume that he realised that his early experience in air fighting was no longer current and on the occasions he did fly, he generally tagged along behind his more experienced flight commanders, as nothing more than a member of the patrol.

He did this on 23 November 1916, taking off from 24's base at Bertangles with two of his pilots. Ironically it would be at Bertangles (see page 145) that von Richthofen would be buried after his death in April 1918.

Over the front the three DH2s were engaged by *Jasta* 2 and after the initial skirmish, Hawker and von Richthofen began an individual dog-fight. Hawker was a fairly able pilot and had a good machine under him although his recent combat experience was not up to the German's. However, von Richthofen was often thought to be a better fighter and tactician than pilot, so their skills were pretty well matched this day.

The fight went on for some time with neither man gaining an advantage in a circling battle. Finally Hawker needed to break off and make a dash for the British lines or risk being forced down into captivity as his fuel gave out. In making this dash, he allowed the German pilot a better target for a burst of fire at his DH2.

What damage was done we shall never know, although we do know that Hawker himself was only hit by a single bullet to the head, which killed him instantly. His body was buried next to the wreckage of his machine, and over time his grave was lost during constant battles across the area.

Much has been made out of this combat, mainly by pulp writers of later years, recording this as some sort of knightly joust of two ace pilots. Von Richthofen had a faster, heavier machine equipped with two belt fed machine guns and hundreds of rounds. Hawker had a single Lewis gun fitted with a drum of ammunition containing 97 rounds. Valuable time was lost each time a drum needed changing and while doing so you were distracted from your opponent's activities. In truth it was a one-sided fight, with Hawker endeavouring to avoid being shot down by turning and using his machine's greater agility.

Major L G Hawker VC DSO, commanding 24 Squadron. Killed in action with the Baron on 23 November 1916 following a long aerial duel. Hawker fell at Luisenhof Farm but his grave was later lost.

At the time, Hawker was not unknown and his death was a sad blow to the RFC – he was about to be given a Wing to command – but in the final analysis he was just another airman of major rank who had fallen. Von Richthofen's name was emerging as someone with potential, but this was, nevertheless, only his eleventh success.

Return north on the D10 through the village then turn left on the C3 to Grevillers. Cross over the D929 and in Grevillers go left on the D29 to Bihucourt, then right on the C6 to Bihucourt. At a T junction turn left on the D7 to Achiet-le-Grand. Follow the D7 through the village and immediately after the railway bridge go right at the green CWGC sign. At the fork bear left and the military cemetery is behind the civil one.

Achiet-le-Grand Communal Cemetery Extension

Achiet-le-Grand has a similar history to Lebuquière. Occupied by the 7/Bedfords on 17 March 1917, it was lost again on 25 March 1918, despite a defence by the 1/6 Manchesters, then remained in German hands until 23 August when it was finally recaptured.

During the first Allied occupation the village was used as a railhead, and was home to the 45th and 49th Casualty Clearing Stations. It was later used to a lesser extent by the Germans, and then again by the Allies until the end of the war. After the armistice further burials took place.

There are four First World War burials within the communal cemetery itself, while the extension has 1,424, of which 200 are unidentified. No less than 35 are flying men and among the earliest are two who were shot down by von Richthofen. The grave of Ian Cameron is on the right-hand side past the Cross of Sacrifice in the front row near the rear cemetery boundary.

John (Ian) Gilmour Cameron (II M 19)

Second Lieutenant J G Cameron, (sometimes recorded as Ian) of 12 Squadron, was shot down in his BE2c on 9 November 1916, the Baron's eighth kill.

His squadron had been ordered to bomb a sugar factory at Vraucourt, just north of Bapaume. Although flying BE2c two-seaters, these machines when used as bombers often flew without an observer in order to carry a larger bomb load. This generally necessitated the use of an escort and indeed this day fighters were on hand but it did not stop *Jasta* 2 from shooting down two, wounding the pilot of another, as well as damaging two of the escorting FEs.

It must have been a large and confused action, as the British force, consisting of 11 Squadron's FEs, 29 Squadron's DH2s and 60 Squadron's scouts, totalled sixteen bombers and fourteen fighters. They were attacked by an estimated thirty German fighters from *Jasta* 1 and *Jasta* 2.

Second Lieutenant J G Cameron of 12 Squadron, shot down on 9 November 1916, dying from his wounds at Beugny Dressing Station. Aged 19.

Von Richthofen caused confusion in his combat report by saying there was an observer on board as well as a pilot, but this is incorrect. John Cameron was flying alone when he was shot down. He was pulled seriously wounded from the wreckage of his aircraft, and died later of his wounds.

John Cameron, who preferred 'Ian', the Scottish form of his Christian name, came from 'The Fountain', Loanhead, near Edinburgh, the elder son of Surgeon Major James and his wife, Mary Cameron. Educated at Leeswade, Edinburgh and the Royal Military College,

Sandhurst, he was a keen sportsman, representing his school at rugby and the shot putt, and Sandhurst at rugby.

He was commissioned into the Cameron Highlanders on 22 December 1915, being posted to France in June 1916. He transferred to the RFC the following January, and gained his Royal Aero Club Aviators Certificate, No. 2624, on 25 March 1917. He then returned to France and was with 12 Squadron when he was killed eight months later.

George Doughty (II M 6)

The next grave we are visiting is in the same row as Cameron but thirteen graves further along towards the cemetery boundary.

In the Porte-de-Paris section of Chapter Three (see page 100) we read the details of the action on 20 November 1916 which resulted in von Richthofen gaining his tenth victory.

Gilbert Hall, the pilot of the 18 Squadron FE2b was seriously wounded, and eventually died of his wounds in a German hospital in Cambrai, his remains now lie in Porte-de-Paris.

His observer, George Doughty, was killed in the action and so was buried apart from his pilot in Achiet-le-Grand. George Doughty, born in 1895, was the son of George and Betty Doughty of 2 Albert Place, Leith Walk, Edinburgh and, like Ian Cameron, was another Scot from Edinburgh.

He was originally commissioned into the 13/(Service) Battalion, the Royal Scots (the old First of Foot) and later transferred to the Royal Flying Corps, joining 18 Squadron on 7 August 1916. He officially qualified as an observer on 9 October 1916, and was then on leave from the 18th to 24th before returning to 18 Squadron just four weeks before his death.

Second Lieutenant G Doughty, 18 Squadron, was observer to G S Hall on 20 November 1916. Unlike his pilot who survived for a further ten days, Doughty died in the crash.

Return to the D7 and turn right then right again to Ablainzville. Pass through the village then turn right on the D919 to Ayette. In the village turn left on the D7 to Douchy-les-Ayette. The cemetery is on the right as you enter the village.

Douchy-les-Ayette British Cemetery

Douchy-les-Ayette was in German hands from the beginning of the war until the retreat to the Hindenburg Line in March 1917. During their spring offensive of 1918 they advanced as far as the communal cemetery across the road from the British cemetery and held it for a few days.

The British cemetery was not started until the summer of 1918, by the 3rd Division Burial Officer when 81 graves were made. It was enlarged after the war with burials from the surrounding battlefields, and graves were moved here from another fourteen cemeteries in the area. There are now over 700 casualties here, some one third being unidentified.

There are eleven airmen among the known, the most notable being a victim of the Red Baron – Gerry Knight DSO MC. His grave is in the third row from the centre aisle on the left side of the cemetery.

Arthur Gerald Knight (III C 11)

Twenty-one-year-old Captain Gerry Knight, was already a British ace, with eight victories to his credit, when he was shot down at 1030 hours on the morning of 20 December 1916 to become von Richthofen's thirteenth victory.

Knight and his colleagues from 29 Squadron had taken off in their DH2s from Le Hameau on an offensive patrol over Rollencourt and Gommecourt some three quarters of an hour earlier. Von Richthofen described in his combat report how he fired on his target from close range hitting the British aircraft, after which it went down and hit the ground. Indeed witnesses behind the British lines saw the aircraft spinning down to crash east of Adinfer Wood. There must have been a considerable scrap between 29 Squadron and

Captain A G Knight DSO MC, 29 Squadron, killed in action 20 December 1916, an experienced pilot with several victories himself.

von Richthofen and his four colleagues, as although Gerry Knight's was the only DH2 shot down, four others were damaged, one making an emergency landing south of Beaumetz, the other three making it back to Le Hameau.

Gerry Knight was born in Bedford on 30 July 1895, his family then moving to Canada, where he completed his education at Toronto University. He later returned to England and lived with relatives at 4 Cambridge Road, Southampton.

He obtained his Royal Aero Club Aviators Certificate, No. 2063, on 11 November 1915, and joined 4 Squadron in France during February 1916. In June he was transferred to 24 Squadron, under the command of the legendary Lanoe Hawker VC DSO. (see page 115)

Knight was indirectly involved in the death of the great German ace Oswald Boelcke when, on the 28 October 1916. He was on patrol with Alfred McKay, also flying a DH2, over the Somme when they were attacked by Boelcke. During the fight Boelcke's aircraft collided with that of his friend and colleague Erwin Böhme, whose undercarriage hit Boelcke's upper wing, and although no immediate damage seemed to have been caused Boelcke's wing broke away and his aircraft crashed.

Gerry Knight continued to fly through the Battle of the Somme, and his qualities may be judged by the award of the Military Cross and then the Distinguished Service Order. The citations for the awards read as follows:-

Military Cross. London Gazette *14 November 1916.*

For conspicuous skill and gallantry. He has shown great pluck in fights with enemy machines, and has accounted for several. On one occasion, when a hostile machine was interfering with a reconnaissance, he attacked at very close range, and brought down the machine in flames.

Distinguished Service Order. London Gazette *11 December 1916.*

For conspicuous gallantry in action. He led four machines against 18 hostile machines. Choosing a good moment for attack he drove down five of them and dispersed the remainder. He has shown the utmost dash and judgement as a leader of offensive patrols.

In November 1916 Knight was transferred to 29 Squadron, who were also operating the DH2, as a flight commander, and continued to do good work, gaining his eighth and last victory just four days before his death, and received a Mention in Despatches (the only honour other than the Victoria Cross which could be given posthumously) in January 1917. He was due to go on leave had he returned from his fatal patrol.

Return to the D919 and turn left for Arras. This concludes the third tour.

Final Days

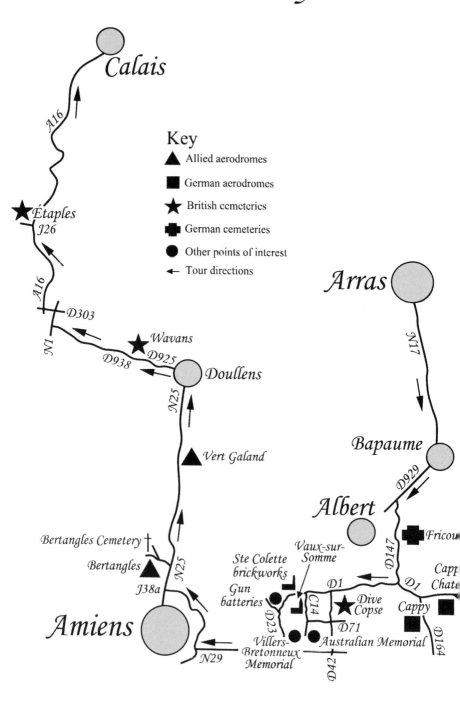

Key
- ▲ Allied aerodromes
- ■ German aerodromes
- ★ British cemeteries
- ✚ German cemeteries
- ● Other points of interest
- ← Tour directions

Calais

A16

Étaples
J26

A16

N1

D303

Wavans
D938   D925

Arras

N17

Doullens

N25

Vert Galand

Bapaume

D929

Albert

D147

Fricou

Bertangles Cemetery †

Bertangles

N25

J38a

Ste Colette
brickworks

Vaux-sur-
Somme

Capp
Chate

Gun
batteries

D1

D1

Cappy

Amiens

D23

C14

Dive
Copse

D71

D164

Villers-
Bretonneux
Memorial

Australian Memorial

N29

D42a

Chapter Four

FINAL DAYS

The final part of *In the Footsteps of the Red Baron* deals predominantly with the last days of von Richthofen's life and in particular the action in which he was killed.

Fricourt German Cemetery – Von Richthofen's second burial site
Cappy German Aerodrome – Von Richthofen's last patrol
Dive Copse British Cemetery – G H Harding
Australian Corps Memorial – View of Morlancourt Ridge
Vaux-sur-Somme – The pursuit of 'Wop' May
Ste Colette Brickworks – Von Richthofen crash site
Corbie – 53 and 55 Batteries Australian Field Artillery
Villers-Bretonneux Australian Memorial – Panoramic views
Bertangles British Aerodrome – 209 Squadron RAF
Bertangles Communal Cemetery – Von Richthofen's first burial site
Vert Galand British Aerodrome – A black day for 19 Squadron
Wavans Military Cemetery – James McCudden VC
Étaples Military Cemetery – F S Seymour, 13 Squadron

Depart Arras on the N17 to Bapaume. Continue until a roundabout and go right on the D929 to Albert. Follow Albert signs round the ring road. Continue on the D929 and in Pozières go left on the D147 to Contalmaison, then left on the D20 sign posted to Bray-sur-Somme. Turn right on the D147 again to Fricourt. The German cemetery is on the left as you enter Fricourt.

Fricourt German Cemetery

This is the only German cemetery located within the area of the 1916 British Battle of Somme. Other German graves are scattered among nearby cemeteries but Fricourt in terms of burials – 17,027 - is the second largest in the *département* of the Somme. (The largest is at Vermandovillers)

It was here than Manfred von Richthofen was originally interred after his initial wartime burial at Bertangles. (see page 145) In 1925 his

Von Richthofen and his father Major Albrecht von Richthofen. Sons with fathers also in the military could not gain a higher rank, thus the Red Baron remained a *Rittmeister* – cavalry captain.

The Richthofen brothers, Lothar and Manfred, in front of a Fokker DrI. Between them they accounted for 120 Allied aircraft.

body was exhumed again and taken to Berlin for a state funeral. When the infamous Berlin Wall was built it was moved again, this time to Wiesbaden where von Richthofen now lies.

Recently with the growing tourism and increase in interest about the First World War the authorities have erected signs and information boards at various points in the area. Outside the cemetery at Fricourt is a notice explaining about von Richthofen and gives other locations on the Somme connected with him. His original grave location is given as 1177, which is situated in the far-right rear corner of the cemetery, though another casualty (Sebastian Paustian) now occupies the plot.

Continue ahead into Fricourt. At a crossroads with the D938 continue ahead on the D147 to Bray-sur-Somme, where you take a left turn on the D1 to Cappy. Follow the D1 through the village up the hill past the château on your left. Once on the level just past the château stop. The Cappy Château aerodrome is on your right (and possibly the left as well). Retrace your steps to Cappy village and at the bottom of the hill turn left on the D164 to Dompierre-Becquincourt. Continue up the hill and where a light railway crosses the road stop the car. Cappy aerodrome occupied the area to your right.

Cappy German Aerodrome

The airfield at Cappy was one of several newly established bases by the Germans as they continued to advance in the spring of 1918, and in fact the location had more than one aerodrome. One was known to the RAF as Cappy and another as Cappy Château.

It was from Cappy where von Richthofen claimed his last victories and departed from on his last, fatal flight on 21 April 1918.

It is believed that Cappy Château aerodrome was used by *Jasta* 5 at one stage and of course, there was the nearby château for the officers, although it is uncertain if von Richthofen actually slept here. The château is still there, its drive behind railings and a gate. It looks like many others; not massive but has two stories and a half submerged basement. The front central entrance once again has steps leading up to the door. There is another entrance to the right side visible as one faces the brick and cement building.

Richthofen moved to Cappy on 11 April 1918. He and *Jasta* 11 (he mostly flew with this unit) had operated from Léchelle for just fifteen

The Cappy Aerodromes

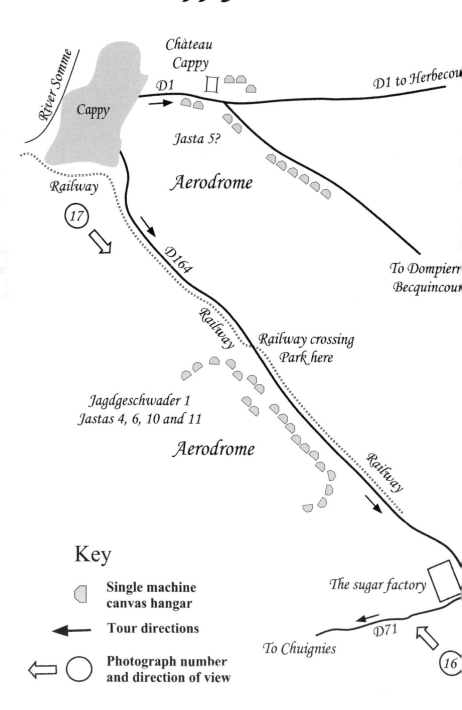

River Somme

Château Cappy

D1

Cappy

D1 to Herbecourt

Jasta 5?

Aerodrome

Railway

17

D164

Railway

To Dompierre Becquincour

Railway crossing Park here

Jagdgeschwader 1
Jastas 4, 6, 10 and 11

Aerodrome

Railway

The sugar factory

Key

Single machine canvas hangar

Tour directions

Photograph number and direction of view

To Chuignies

D71

16

Photograph No. 16: Cappy looking north from the sugar factory in 2003.

Photograph No. 17: Cappy looking south in 2003.

The château at Cappy taken in the late 1990s.

days but the Baron had claimed ten British aircraft shot down – victories 69 to 78 – so it could be said he was virtually back on form, having claimed no victories in December, January and February. However, he must have been feeling tired by this time, particularly having to move his unit frequently.

These ten machines comprised four Camels, two RE8s, two AWKF8s, one SE5a and a Dolphin. Seven of these were fighters and two of the downed Camels' pilots were minor aces, Captain T S Sharpe DFC of 73 Squadron and Captain S P Smith of 46 Squadron. So much for those who say von Richthofen only fought obsolete, easy to shoot down aircraft.

Nevertheless, was it von Richthofen's fault that the RFC/RAF had continued to send inferior machines out to do battle?

Lieutenant R G H Adams of 73 Squadron became victory No.78 on 7 April 1918, although the Baron misidentified his Camel for a Spad. In later life Ronald Adam (his stage name) became a well known actor, appearing in scores of films. He lived to be aged 82.

Tom Sharpe

Captain Thomas Sydney Sharpe is now acknowledged to have been von Richthofen's seventy-first victory, when he was shot down in his 73 Squadron Sopwith Camel, the aircraft falling into the flooded valley of the River Ancre on the morning of 27 March 1918. His is the only Camel loss on that date to match the particulars of von Richthofen's combat report.

Sharpe took off from Remaisnil, northwest of Doullens, where 73 Squadron had been evacuated to from Cachy three day before, on a low level bombing and strafing patrol against the advancing German armies.

Sharpe was wounded in the encounter and spent the rest of the war in captivity, but never acknowledged being shot down by a German pilot, believing his demise was due to ground

Another British ace downed by the Baron, Captain T S Sharpe DFC of 73 Squadron, taken prisoner 27 March 1918.

fire. Whether he did not like to admit that a German got him, or was totally unaware of the Baron's attack, we shall never know.

Tom Sharpe was born in Gloucester on 24 February 1889. Commissioned into the 3/(Reserve) Battalion, the Gloucester Regiment on 17 April 1915, he obtained his Royal Aero Club Aviators Certificate, No. 2471, on 19 February 1916, after which he formally transferred to the RFC. He served in 24 Squadron between May and July 1916, flying DH2s, receiving rapid promotion to captain and eventually became a flight commander with 73 Squadron. By the end of March 1918 Sharpe had scored six victories, and thus was an ace. He was one of the first people to receive the newly instituted Distinguished Flying Cross, which was gazetted some six months after his capture. The citation reads:-

A gallant officer who has always led his patrol with marked skill and judgement. On one occasion he chased down an Albatros scout and caused it to crash. He afterwards attacked five enemy machines destroying two. On the following day, encountering four Albatros scouts, he engaged one, which crashed. Proceeding on his patrol, he met a formation of enemy scouts; he chased one and destroyed it.

Tom Sharpe was repatriated in December 1918 and returned to civilian life. He lived at Courtthorpe, Tuffley, Gloucester where for many years he ran a building company.

Sydney Philip Smith

Captain Sydney Philip Smith, of 46 Squadron, became von Richthofen's seventy-sixth victim, when he was shot down just over a week after Tom Sharpe, in the afternoon of 6 April 1918. Like Sharpe, Smith was flying a Sopwith Camel, and also like Sharpe, was engaged on strafing ground targets when the Baron attacked him. No sooner had von Richthofen begun firing than he saw the Camel begin to leave a trail of flame and smoke, then crash to earth on fire.

Philip Smith, as he liked to be called, signing himself 'S Philip Smith', was born on 10 May 1896, the son of Mr and Mrs Arthur Smith of 'Morningside', Cargate, Aldershot, Hampshire. Educated at King's College, Wimbledon, he was a member of the school's OTC for over four years, and captained the school's rifle team at the annual Public School's 'Shooting Blue Ribbon' at Bisley.

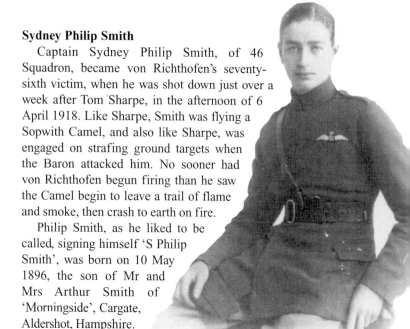

Captain S P Smith, 46 Squadron, shot down by the Baron on 6 April 1918, for victory No.76. He has no known grave.

He enlisted as a private in the Public Schools Battalion as soon as war began, and was soon selected for a commission, being gazetted into the Army Service Corps on 21 October 1914. By March 1915 he was in France and was eventually allowed to transfer to the RFC in June 1916, having gained his Royal Aero Club Aviators Certificate, No. 3056, on 24 May.

Smith joined 6 Squadron in France on 22 June, and his skill on the BE2 was such that by the end of the year he had been made flight commander. On 26 January 1917 he was involved in an action in which he was slightly wounded, although his observer, Lieutenant Handsworth was more seriously injured, having to have his right arm amputated as a result of the wounds he received. On 1 May, during another hectic action, his fourth flight of the day, he was shot down, but managed to force land his damaged aircraft on the British side of the lines alongside 15 Heavy Battery near Reninghelst.

128

On 6 March 1918 he was posted to 46 Squadron as a flight commander and between then and his death, exactly a month later he shot down four aircraft, which with his previous victory made him an ace. His commanding officer, Major R H S Mealing described Philip Smith as '*wonderfully brave, perhaps too brave*'. Whether this bravery resulted in his pressing on too long against his ground targets so that he did not see the six approaching aircraft of *Jasta* 11 we will never know.

There is a remarkable story concerning the death of Philip Smith. The Baron's combat report noted that his Camel had crashed '*near the little wood north-east of Villers-Bretonneux, where it continued burning on the ground*'.

Smith's father was able to go to France after the war in company with Donald Gold who had flown with No.3 Squadron – also equipped with Sopwith Camels – and who had actually been shot down in the same area shortly before Smith was brought down. Gold was claimed by one of von Richthofen's men, Hans Kirschstein of *Jasta* 6, north-east of Wartisse, his fifth of an eventual 27 victories.

Once on the ground, Gold had seen the red Triplane shoot down the Camel which exploded in flames and fell to the ground. He was able to take Arthur Smith to the location mapping the area and together they actually found various pieces of the wreckage from the Camel, but they were unable to locate any form of grave that might have held his son's mortal remains. Philip Smith is commemorated on the Arras Memorial to the Missing.

At this final stage of the Baron's career, his four *jagdstaffeln* were commanded by the following. *Jasta* 4 – *Leutnant* Kurt Wüsthoff (27 victories); *Jasta* 6 – *Oberleutnant* Wilhelm Reinhard (12 victories); *Jasta* 10 – *Leutnant* Erich Löwenhardt (15 victories); *Jasta* 11 – *Leutnant* Hans Weiss (14 victories). Von Richthofen's personal score was by this time 78.

His mother was hoping he would soon decide to take a prolonged rest from flying following the arduous time he had had during the March offensive and there does seem to have been some movement by the top brass to order him to either rest or have a total break from operations.

What exactly was in the mind of von Richthofen is difficult to surmise. He knew he was tiring yet his dedication to the war and to his men was paramount. Perhaps he mentally thought a score of 80 – twice that of his friend and mentor Oswald Boelcke – might be a good moment, or, having scored ten in recent days, why not get to the 100 mark and then quit?

Significantly he did not score any more victories between 7 and 20 April 1918. Mostly this was due to bad spring weather but even when flying was possible, *JG* I made very few claims. The time was spent by the ground troops in preparing for the new attack on the Somme.

The front lines here were not all trenches and barbed wire and in the main Australian troops held this sector. There was a series of strong points and in between the gaps, machine-gun crews which had dug themselves into camouflaged and sheltered positions. The Germans too only had a series of strong points with gaps linked by barbed wire and machine-guns.

There were several RAF squadrons opposing the Germans in this sector. At Bertangles (see page 144) there was a Sopwith Camel unit, 209 Squadron RAF, which had been 9 Naval Squadron before the RFC and RNAS had merged just three weeks earlier, on 1 April 1918. Just to the south at another part of the aerodrome, which was known as Poulainville, were the RE8s of No.3 Squadron, Australian Flying Corps. Until recently, 3 AFC also had had an advanced strip on top of the Morlancourt Ridge, not far from Welcome Wood. Both units were to figure in von Richthofen's last flight.

Von Richthofen's last victories

On 20 April part of *JG* I was in the air south of the Somme and they attacked a patrol of Sopwith Camels from 3 Squadron RAF. In the encounter von Richthofen shot down two of them.

First to go down was the squadron commander, although, like Hawker before him, he was not leading, but following the lead of his senior flight commander. Major Richard Raymond-Barker MC, another experienced British airman, although probably not up to par with April 1918 fighting tactics, fell in flames just north of what is now the E44. (see page 86 The Arras Memorial).

Moments later the Baron despatched another Camel from the same unit, this one flown by Second Lieutenant D G Lewis, a Rhodesian. He was luckier and managed to crash, 50 yards from the wrecked and burning Camel of his CO. As he scrambled from the wreck, a Fokker Triplane zoomed past, its pilot waving. If this was the Baron, celebrating his 80th victory, it is understandable, but he may have thought Lewis was in fact a German soldier, as he later reported that both

Second Lieutenant D G Lewis, the Baron's 80th and final victory, taken prisoner on 20 April 1918. From Rhodesia, he was 19 years old but lived to be 79, thus lasting sixty years after his encounter with Germany's highest scoring fighter ace.

British airmen would have died in the fight. Von Richthofen, in waving to a 'soldier' was making sure someone on the ground would be able to help confirm his latest victories by seeing his all-red Fokker.

In overall terms we have von Richthofen's nine final victories all downed in this general area, seven north of the E44, two to the south, and all scored between 27 March and 20 April 1918.

Return to Bray-sur-Somme and turn right on the D329 to Albert, then go left on the D1 to Corbie. Shortly after the junction with the D42 and Beacon Cemetery on the left you will see a green CWGC sign to Dive Copse British Cemetery. Turn left and the cemetery will appear also appear on the left.

Dive Copse British Cemetery

In June 1916, before the Battle of the Somme, the area just to the north of the cemetery was chosen as a concentration point for field ambulances, eventually becoming the XIV Corps Main Dressing Station. Originally Dive Copse was a title given to a small wood, named after the officer commanding the dressing station. The cemetery was begun during the first three months of the Somme campaign in 1916, but was abandoned during the spring battles of 1918. It was retaken in August of that year and a further 77 burials are the result of this fighting.

Much later the site was extended as scattered graves were exhumed and the bodies brought to this location, in particular the casualties from Essex Cemetery, Sailly-le-Sec, begun by the 10/Essex Regiment in August 1918. Today there are 589 graves here, all but 30 being identified.

There are only three RFC graves, one as the result of von Richthofen. The grave of George Harding is at the far right corner in a distinctive group of three headstones.

George Helliwell Harding (I D 7)

Second Lieutenant G H Harding, was an American, aged 24, from South Minneapolis, Minnesota and was shot down by the Baron on 27 March 1918 in a Dolphin of 79 Squadron. He had taken off from Beauvois, to the east of Hesdin, at 1530 hours on an offensive patrol. The Baron misidentified the Dolphin with its twin-bay wings, as a Bristol Fighter, missing the fact that there was only one occupant instead of the normal two, by assuming the observer's cockpit had been covered over. Perhaps his mistake was understandable, as the Dolphin was a type new to the Front. Harding's aircraft was victory number 73, and one of three von Richthofen shot down this day.

Of interest is that Harding, like so many dead aviators discovered in burnt-out wrecks, was buried as totally unknown and unidentified. Richthofen noted the fall of the craft as one kilometre north of Chuignolles, south of Bray-sur-Somme. Chuignolles is just south of the Somme canal, due south of Bray, with Cappy just to the east.

The vast majority of grieving relatives never had the chance of seeking out missing graves of their loved ones and had to rely on post-war investigations and the final resting places given to them by the Imperial War Graves Commission. Only then – if they had been found in the first place - could they visit the grave.

However, in George Harding's case his sister Ruth was in France with a drama company, entertaining the troops. Although it was more than a year after her brother's death, she set out to find where he had been buried.

Following several attempts she finally discovered a small graveyard in the area in which there were a number of unidentified airmen. Somehow this remarkable lady managed to persuade officials at the Imperial War Graves Commission to disinter the remains, and she was able to identify one as her brother. He was then moved to a marked grave in Dive Copse.

George Harding had been born in September 1893, the son of Grain Commissioner George P Harding and his wife Mary, of 1815 Colefax Avenue South, Minneapolis, Minnesota, USA. Educated locally at West High School, Minneapolis, he then joined the firm of E S Woodworth & Co, the company where his father was vice-president.

When the USA entered the war in April 1917, George volunteered for the US Army, but was disappointed to find that demand was such that he would not be trained for some time. Rather than wait, he travelled to Canada and there joined the Royal Flying Corps.

He soon gained his wings, and within weeks was, in turn, instructing novice pilots. In the autumn of 1917 he enjoyed a short

embarkation leave, and then left for England. After further training he was posted to 73 Squadron at Beauvois in March 1918.

George Harding's grave carries an unusual epitaph: *That their dust may rebuild a nation and their souls relight a star.*

Continue ahead into Sailly-Laurette. At a T junction go left, then right on the D42 towards Lamotte-Warfusée. Turn right on the D71 to Le Hamel. The road is paralleling the valley and the Australian Corps Memorial can be seen on the horizon to the left. Just after entering the village there is a sign for the memorial park to the left. Turn left up the hill to the memorial.

The Australian Corps Memorial

There are two very good spots from where to view almost the whole panorama of the Morlancourt Ridge. It was along the valley of the Somme and over the Morlancourt Ridge that Richthofen pursued 'Wop' May of 209 Squadron RAF and where Richthofen was fatally shot and brought down on 21 April 1918. For details of the last flight see page 137.

The first vantage point is here, the Australian Corps Memorial which has been constructed in recent years. It has a large black marble memorial upon which plaques of the Australian units that fought around here are mounted. Behind the area are some excavated German trenches.

From here you can see the church spire of La Hamel seemingly rising out of the ground just to the west and then all the salient points involved in the Baron's last flight including the crash site at Ste Colette.

Looking north and north-west across the Somme canal, virtually the

Panorama of the Morlancourt Ridge showing the chimney of the Ste. Colette brickworks, taken from the Australian Corps Memorial site just east of Le Hamel.

whole length of the ridge stretches across the immediate horizon.

Interestingly, there exists an aerial photograph of this area taken by one of the two RE8 machines of 3 Australian Squadron just moments before they were engaged by von Richthofen and his pilots. This was only a short while before the Germans became embroiled with the Camels of 209 Squadron. Had one been standing at the spot where this Australian Memorial is located and looked straight up (and smiled!) you would have been 'caught on camera'. (see page 26 in *The Red Baron's Last Flight*.)

Return down the hill and turn left. Follow the road through the village past the church on the D71. Continue ahead through Vaire-sous-Corbie on the C202 towards Vaux-sur-Somme and bear right at a fork out of the village to cross the canal. Proceed ahead into Vaux-sur-Somme, crossing the D233 and park by the church on the left.

Vaux-sur-Somme

While in the general area, one might like to drive through this village. The crossroads at Vaux with its church are easy to locate. It is this church and tower which 'Wop' May nearly had von Richthofen collide with as he was being pursued relentlessly.

May had swerved to the right and headed for the Morlancourt Ridge, and Richthofen, chasing hard with some of his concentration directed at his malfunctioning guns, did not see the church tower till the last moment.

Continue up the hill on the C14 towards Méricourt l'Abbé. At the crossroads turn left on the D1 to Fouilly and Corbie. You will soon see the chimney of the disused Ste Colette brickworks on your right. Park just past these buildings.

The Sainte Colette Brickworks and the Morlancourt Ridge

In early April German troops had begun to move into the area around Le Hamel, just south of the Somme but north of what is now the long straight E44 road. Le Hamel itself is in something of a dip but its church spire position could be clearly seen and a German observation post was positioned in the tower.

THE SOMME RIVER

WELCOME WOOD

CHIMNEY

Park here

THE BRICKWORKS

VON RICHTHOFEN
CRASHED HERE

The brickworks from the air, looking east, although in 1918 the chimney was nearer to the road. On his way back from the site of the Australian field artillery, the Baron came towards the south of the brickworks from the bottom right of this picture. Hit from gunfire from the downwards slope of the ridge to the right, he made his forced landing roughly in the middle of the large field area south-west of the chimney.

To the north-west the Morlancourt Ridge stretches away to the west and the Somme twists and turns below it. To the south, where the river and the ridge bend to the south, sits Corbie on the hillside.

On the other side of the ridge, to the north-west from roughly the bend, is an area of sloping meadow land beyond a small quarry. As these meadows slip away to the north-east bound D120 road from Corbie to Mericourt, with the Ancre River beyond, the Australian 53rd and 55th Field Artillery Batteries had selected a spot in order to fire unseen towards the concentration of troops and supplies in Le Hamel.

With the weather starting to improve on the 20 April 1918, *JG* I was given a task. The two Australian gun batteries needed to be urgently located and photographed by German reconnaissance machines and to do this a degree of local air superiority had to be obtained. *JG* I had been sent south in order to assist the coming offensive over the Somme area, and this was the first time any real objective had been given them since arriving.

A secondary responsibility, but none the less important, was to keep British reconnaissance aircraft from looking too closely at Le Hamel, although much of what was happening could be seen through field glasses from the Morlancourt Ridge.

Leader of *Jasta* 11, Hans Weiss with his Triplane. His aircraft was damaged in the fight with the RE8s before the final battle with 209 Squadron's Camels.

Baron von Richthofen playing with Moritz minutes before the final take-off on the morning of 21 April 1918.

Von Richthofen's last flight

We now come to the fateful 21 April 1918. Towards late morning von Richthofen led a patrol of *Jasta* 11, with Hans Weiss from their aerodrome at Cappy (see page 124) and over the front they engaged two RE8s of 3 AFC. In the skirmish that ensued, Weiss's Triplane was hit and damaged, and he flew back to Cappy. Von Richthofen had one of his twin Spandau guns jam and the other suffered a split firing pin which gave him trouble, firing intermittently while he had to pull back the cocking handle each time it failed. To help his movement in the cockpit he released his shoulder harness.

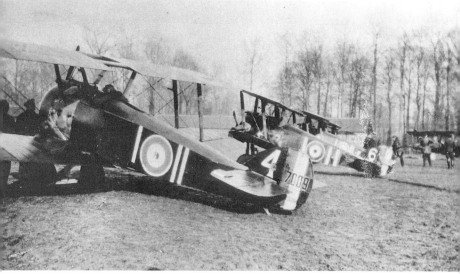

Sopwith Camels of 209 Squadron.

At this moment, the Camels of 209 Squadron appeared in the area. The fight with the RE8s had ended and the Fokker Triplanes had re-formed. A squadron-strength formation of Camels – fifteen aircraft – had flown out to patrol the front but one flight had become detached in cloud. The others then engaged two Albatros C-type, or two-seater, reconnaissance planes. The now ten-man patrol headed north and spotted the Triplanes, following which a fight began.

There is no need to go fully into the action which resulted in the death of the Baron. Anyone who has not read *The Red Baron's Last Flight* by Norman Franks and Alan Bennett (see the Further Reading section) is urged to do so in order to fully understand the circumstances of his

'Wop' May who narrowly escaped becoming von Richthofen's 81st victim on 21 April 1918.

loss. As is well known, von Richthofen chased the Camel flown by Second Lieutenant W R (Wop) May as he broke from the fight and headed low and fast towards Bertangles and home. The Baron spotted him and gave chase. May, desperately trying to avoid gunfire from Richthofen's guns, was twisting and turning and in Vaux-sur-Somme narrowly missed the church tower. (see page 134)

Having become disorientated as to his exact position and because he was having to cope with his gun problems, von Richthofen is believed to have mistakenly flown into Allied territory. By the time he realised this, and taking into account his gun problems, then, once he had failed to down May as they flew over Morlancourt Ridge, he decided to turn back. One has to wonder too, if the Baron had realised the gun batteries were hidden behind the ridge, particularly when he came under direct fire from the Australian's defensive machine guns.

As the Baron turned east to head back towards his own lines, he was hit by ground fire and fatally wounded, being forced to crash-land in a sugar beat field in front of the Sainte Colette brickworks on top of the ridge. That he landed still alive we know from the soldier who first reached the Triplane, and saw him expire. From that, and the knowledge of his wound, we can calculate how long he could have survived after being hit.

There are several points of interest to see in this area. It is known that many visitors have taken *The Red Baron's Last Flight* with them to study the terrain and the points of interest as they stand in various spots indicated.

The road along the top of the Ridge is a must-place to drive along and to stop. This is the D1 running from Corbie eastwards towards Bray-sur-Somme. The brickworks chimney, incidentally, is no longer in its 1918 position being now further back from the road. At the time of writing it is beginning to look a little unsafe and in fact a number of bricks from the top courses have fallen down.

There are several cottages here and the field in which the Red Baron force/crash-landed is due south, some 100 yards from the road. The site of the old quarry, which was off to the right in 1918, is now merely a bunch of low trees and shrubs – looking every bit like a small copse.

Still looking south the terrain slowly drops away, and while one cannot see it from here, the Somme River and Canal are at the bottom of this slope. Way off to the left are the trees of Welcome Wood near to where a forward artillery observation post first saw the two Camels and the triplane heading low along the canal.

The second Camel was flown by Captain Roy Brown DSC of 209 Squadron who had spotted May in trouble with a triplane chasing him and had dived to help. He had converged on the two aircraft from across the Somme, using the southern sun behind him and the morning mist over the canal to help hide his approach, as an experienced fighter pilot would do. He opened fire on the triplane more in hope of distracting the German pilot than hitting him, and in some measure he succeeded.

Von Richthofen now not only had his gun problems but another Camel to contend with. However, such was the angle of approach by Brown that he had to haul his Camel round to the east and for some moments lost sight of the two aeroplanes. On this late morning of 21 April 1918, the sun was shining at an angle of 23 degrees above the horizon, and brightly above the low mist over

Captain A R Brown DSC, 209 Squadron. He chased the Baron, who was pursuing 'Wop' May westwards along the Somme valley towards Corbie with the Morlancourt Ridge off to their right.

the Somme. Had von Richthofen turned to the left (south) and into the attack of the second Camel (Brown) he would have been blinded, which is no doubt why he turned to the right and possibly seeing Brown begin a turn left towards Corbie, continued after May.

The distraction, meantime, helped May gain some small distance ahead of his pursuer and it was now that von Richthofen, aware of the danger he was in, realised as he crested the ridge and came under machine-gun fire from the Australians of the two batteries, his exact location and decided it was time to leave. Hauling round to the right to the east he was low and very vulnerable. Moments later he was hit, most probably by an experienced machine gunner situated just above the canal and below the level of the ridge.

It will never be known if Sergeant Cedric Popkin fired the bullet that mortally wounded the Red Baron. Today, he is credited with having done so because he had the best chance, was an expert shot, knew exactly how to 'lead' his target, and was the only man found that fired at the Triplane from the appropriate side – the aircraft's right. Everyone else known to have fired at it, fired from either the left side, left rear, or from the front. See the next entry, the site of the Australian Batteries.

Return on the D1 towards Corbie. As you go down the hill turn right on the D23 to Bonnay. There is a statue/memorial on the right in the fork of the road. A few hundred yards after the turn stop in a long layby on your right.

The Site of the Australian Batteries on 21 April 1918

To your right is a wood and between you and it is the road you have just driven down from the brickworks. This meadow between the two roads is in the lee of the ridge.

Hidden from the German positions, therefore, on the reverse (north-western) slope of the ridge, sat the gun batteries of the 53rd and 55th Field Artillery units. It was these guns that the Germans were anxious to locate in mid-April 1918, and thus were the reason *JG* I had been tasked with providing air cover so that two-seaters could try to find them. Two members of these batteries, cooks trained as Lewis gunners in the event of air attack, named Robert Buie and William Evans, had fired at the Baron's triplane as it chased May over the Ridge.

Did von Richthofen, in his last moments of life, spot the guns and

The position of the Australian batteries looking north. From here they were able to fire shells into the German positions beyond the Morlancourt Ridge.

realise he had found what they had been searching for? Is that why he gave up the chase and turned right (east) to head back to the German lines, or had he merely given up the struggle with a final curse at his troublesome guns? We shall never know. Seconds later, as he headed back over the ridge, with the brickworks coming up to his left, he was hit.

A single .303 bullet came through the right-hand side of the triplane's cockpit and entered his side. Like a painful dig in the ribs, he jerked his right arm back and in so doing the nose of his fighter suddenly pitched upwards. Way off to the right, down by the Somme canal, a sergeant who had watched the events as he worked on a pontoon bridge, saw the German aeroplane rise suddenly, then plunge downwards. '*It was like someone hitting a brick wall*', the soldier recalled.

The bullet had penetrated the body, hit and then been deflected forward off the spine, ripping either through the back of the heart or the aorta. Having slowed considerably in doing so, it only had the power to exit the chest below the left nipple but not to continue through the Baron's leather flying jacket.

The bullet had come from the right. Virtually everyone who has been identified as firing at the triplane fired either from the left side, the left-rear, or the front. Only Sergeant Popkin just below the ridge off to the

Baron's right, had fired from the correct side. He was an experienced machine gunner and knew how to 'lead' a target, which he would have to have done at the range of 600 yards. Ballistics too indicate that at 600 yards bullets do not break up but go through flesh fairly cleanly and remain intact, and a bullet was later found in the lining of the Baron's jacket.

He knew he had been hit badly and there was no thought of doing anything but getting himself and his machine down – and quickly. In his last moments all his training came instinctively in a natural progression. He instantly switched off the engine, depressurised the fuel tank and regained partial control. He was already low down and it only took moments for him to crunch down onto the stubble field. As his fighter slowed, the undercarriage smashed into a pile of beet and was ripped away, but the Fokker remained upright. Then sudden silence. Perhaps the ticking of cooling hot metal. Some dust in the air and in the cockpit.

Within moments, the face of a soldier appeared by his machine. The Baron knew he had been fatally hit. He mumbled something in German, like – '*I've had it,*' and died.

Turn round and continue in to Corbie on the D1. Follow signs to Fouilly and Villers-Bretonneux, cross over the canal then turn left on the D23 to Villers-Bretonneux. The memorial will appear on the left.

The Australian Memorial at Villers-Bretonneux

The second observation point for von Richthofen's fight, the first is from the Australian Corps Memorial (see page 133), is in the Australian Memorial and cemetery at Villers-Bretonneux.

Its steps lead up from a car-parking area. Cresting the top of the steps one sees a broad avenue of open ground, a huge cross at its centre, and either side amidst two rows of trees are numerous headstones to the fallen.

Having walked through this area one has already seen the tall tower at the far end. Inside there is a large open stairwell. Climb to the observation area at the top of the building for a fine view of the surrounding countryside.

Lamotte-Warfusee to the south-east, on the Amiens to St. Quentin road, is of interest because above here Lieutenant R G H Adams of 73 Squadron was shot down on 7 April 1918 to become the Baron's

A view from the top of the tower of the Australian Memorial. To the left of the Morlancourt Ridge is the town of Corbie and on the right can be seen the chimney of the Ste Colette brickworks.

78th victory. For a long time the identity of this victory was uncertain simply because the Baron claimed an English Spad. By this date the RAF no longer had Spads in France and in fact he had confused his victim with a Camel. Von Richthofen and another *JG* I pilot, Hans Kirschstein of *Jasta* 6, claimed the same machine, and having correctly identified it as a Camel, also received credit. Adams crashed and appeared dead to the German soldiers on the ground, who had in fact thrown a tarpaulin over his body. Only when Adams moaned did they discover the British airman was hurt but far from dead.

To the west the city of Amiens is in the distance, a tempting target for the Germans in the First World War but one never attained.

Looking north and north-east, across open farmland the whole Morlancourt Ridge lays open to view a little over a mile away. In the middle distance are the lines of trees which mark the meandering Somme. Immediately to the north are the buildings of Foilloy and across the Somme, Corbie. Atop of the ridge, to the north-east is the gaunt black marker where von Richthofen died – the chimney of the Sainte Colette brickworks.

Continue south on the D23 to Villers-Bretonneux then turn right on the N29 to Amiens. At the Amiens ring road follow the N29 then N25 to Amiens. Continue on the N25 and leave at junction 38a to Doullens. Take a left turn to Bertangles. In the village pick up the D97 to Vaux-en-Amiénois and pass through the village. You will reach a railway crossing shortly and park here.

Bertangles British Aerodrome

Bertangles is arguably the most famous British aerodrome on the Western Front and being farmland remains untouched. The features of the aerodrome can be seen from the diagram of the site. More significant incidents occurred here than at any other British aerodrome. Gilbert Insall of 11 Squadron earned his VC while flying from here. Lanoe Hawker VC departed from this spot for his fatal meeting with von Richthofen. 209 Squadron took off from here for their encounter with the Baron and this was where his body and machine were brought.

We come now to the aftermath of the morning actions of 21 April 1918. Once the identity of the German pilot became known, the red triplane was completely souvenired until it was reduced to a few pieces of wreckage. The body was taken to one side and later transported to the airfield at Poulainville, by a party from 3 AFC that had been sent out to collect the triplane.

The well known photographs of personnel standing by or sifting through the wreckage of the triplane were taken the next day. An Army Film Unit also arrived and took a motion film of it.

Photograph No. 18: Bertangles looking north-east in July 2001.

The Bertangles Aerodromes

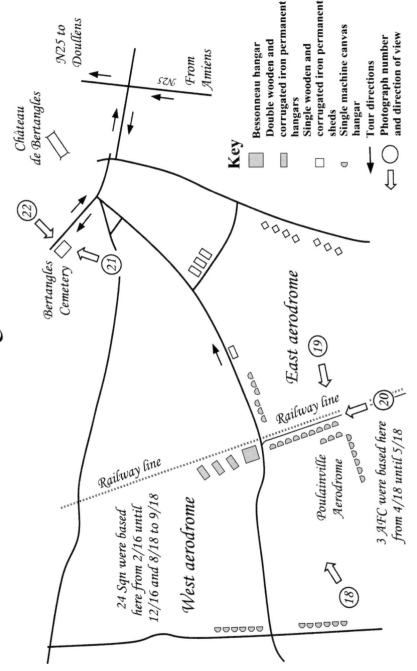

Key

- Bessonneau hangar
- Double wooden and corrugated iron permanent hangars
- Single wooden and corrugated iron permanent sheds
- Single machine canvas hangar
- Tour directions
- Photograph number and direction of view

N25 to Doullens

N25

From Amiens

Château de Bertangles

Bertangles Cemetery

East aerodrome

Railway line

Railway line

West aerodrome

Poulainville Aerodrome

24 Sqn were based here from 2/16 until 12/16 and 8/18 to 9/18

3 AFC were based here from 4/18 until 5/18

(18) (19) (20) (21) (22)

Photograph No. 19: The wreckage of von Richthofen's Fokker Triplane after it had been taken back to Poulainville.

On the evening of the 21st, von Richthofen's body was 'cleaned up' – that is, an orderly wiped some of the blood from the face and chin and then a photographer gently put some baking powder on the damaged area, suffered as the Baron hit his face on the gun butts. He also eased the two front teeth back into position, forced back by the impact. The body was lashed to a trestle, stood upright against the wall

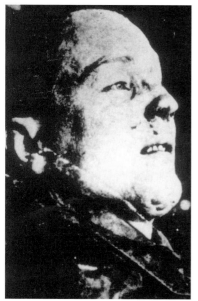

of the hangar and photographed. Also at Poulainville that same evening, the first medical examinations were made of the body and the bullet wound.

In the late afternoon of the following day von Richthofen's body was taken by Crossley Tender from 3 AFC's hangars to the communal cemetery in Bertangles village.

For a fuller account of Bertangles aerodrome see *Airfields and Airmen: Somme*, page 69.

The corpse of the Red Baron, photographed while lashed to a corrugated iron sheet prior to the medical examination.

Photograph No 20: The procession taking the body of von Richthofen to the cemetery at Bertangles village on the late afternoon of 22 April.

Retrace your route to the centre of the village and at a corner which has an iron crucifix turn left and the village cemetery will appear on the left.

Bertangles Communal Cemetery

Bertangles village was virtually taken over by the RFC in the Great War. Nos.13 and 14 Wings had their headquarters here during the Battle of the Somme. Lanoe Hawker VC was based here too with his 24 Squadron in 1916 and their 'A' Flight Mess was at the end of the road coming from the N25.

Von Richthofen was initially buried with full military honours in the afternoon of 22 April. There have been many photographs published of the ceremony, not to mention a motion film, but all have been taken looking at the gates of the cemetery from inside the cemetery as the coffin is brought in and then lowered into the prepared grave. This is followed by the firing of a final salute over the burial spot.

Visiting the burial ground today, the well-known brick gate posts are still there, but it is interesting to look around and see the vista, not shown in wartime photographs. So look directly in the opposite

Photograph No. 21: The service in Bertangles cemetery showing the Australian guard of honour with rifles reversed.

Photograph No. 22: Bertangles cemetery today from outside the gates. The original grave site was just inside to the left. The village can be seen in the background.

direction for a moment. Up the slope a short distance was where the airfield was in the First World War and from where Roy Brown and the others of 209 took off that day.

Von Richthofen's grave was desecrated a number of times with the cross being stolen. His body was eventually removed to the German cemetery at Fricourt (see page 121) before finally returning to Germany in 1925.

Return to the centre of the village and follow the D97 to Villers-Bocage. As you leave the village the imposing château can be seen on the left. At the N25 turn left. After passing the la Vicogne sign farm buildings can be seen on the horizon. Stop a few hundred yards short of these.

Vert Galand British Aerodrome

Vert Galand is probably today the most recognisable British aerodrome from the First World War as the farm which it surrounded has barely changed in the last 85 years. It was in continuous use from 1915 until early 1919. It was first occupied by 4 and 11 Squadrons RFC in July 1915 and many squadrons were based here. Initially only the area east of the Amiens – Doullens road was used but by the end of the war even the area to the north of the farm was employed.

Albert Ball VC, Britain's first air hero took off from here on 7 May 1917 and crashed to his death at Annouellin, north-east of Lens. His squadron, No. 56, formed part of 9 Headquarters Wing, which was moved around the British front bolstering local air operations as the situation dictated. It was used in much the same way as von Richthofen's *Jagdgeschwader.*

Another unit in 9 Wing was 19 Squadron who were flying the

Photograph No. 23: Vert Galand looking south in July 2001.

EAST AERODROME   WEST AERODROME

BARN

1918 AERODROME

Vert Galand Aerodrome

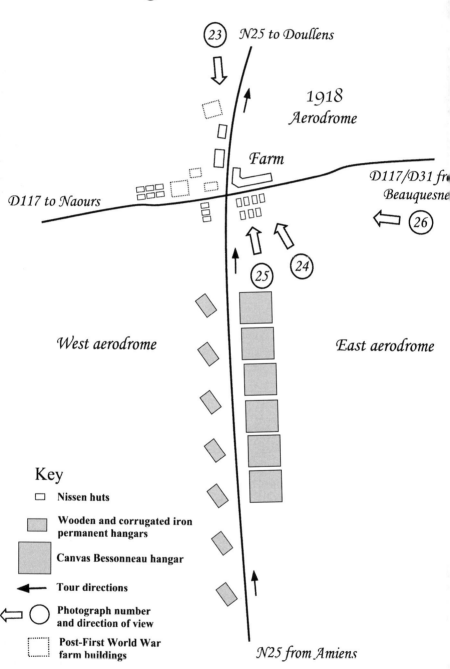

23 N25 to Doullens

1918
Aerodrome

Farm

D117/D31 fr
Beauquesne

D117 to Naours

26

24

25

West aerodrome

East aerodrome

Key

☐ Nissen huts

▦ Wooden and corrugated iron permanent hangars

▦ Canvas Bessonneau hangar

← Tour directions

⇦ ◯ Photograph number and direction of view

⬚ Post-First World War farm buildings

N25 from Amiens

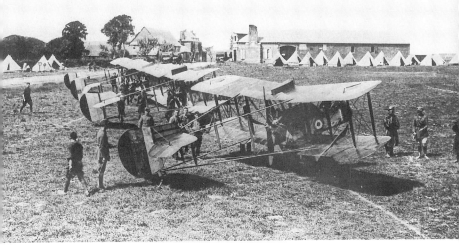

Photograph No. 24: The DH2s of 32 Squadron at Vert Galand in 1916.

French-built Spad fighter. It was commanded by the legendary H D Harvey-Kelly, the first British airman to land in France. On 29 April 1917, little more than a week before Ball's loss, Harvey-Kelly took off from the eastern aerodrome leading two other Spads. All three machines failed to return with two pilots killed and one taken prisoner. Harvey-Kelly is buried in Brown's Copse Cemetery, near Arras and Richard Applin, who was von Richthofen's 49th victim, is commemorated on the Arras memorial. (see page 85)

Photograph No. 25: The farm building at Vert Galand as one approaches the crossroads heading north.

Photograph No. 26: Vert Galand from the east. This 1918 photo shows how the aerodrome has expanded since 1916 with wooden and metal buildings and huts. The line of bell tents have long gone.

Continue north on the N25. In Doullens from the first roundabout pick up the D925 to Abbeville, then the D938 to Auxi-le-Chateau. After leaving Beauvoir-Wavans and passing the junction with the D117 a green CWGC sign will be seen. Turn right up the lane and the cemetery is on the left.

Wavans Military Cemetery

Wavans was the burial ground of the 21st Casualty Clearing Station between May and September 1918 and within it are 43 Commonwealth war dead plus one German.

It is perhaps the ultimate small cemetery on the Western Front. Now a scene of complete tranquillity, the contrast with those years of warfare could not be more marked. And within its tiny area there are a dozen airmen interred here, among them two famous air fighters, James McCudden VC and Robert Little of the Royal Naval Air Service.

McCudden's grave is at the right hand end of the second row and the VC on the headstone makes it stand out from a considerable distance. That of Little is just two rows behind McCudden, his grave engraved with the 'fouled anchor' of the Royal Navy.

Jimmy McCudden VC (B 10)

Here is the great Major J T B McCudden VC, DSO & Bar, MC & Bar, MM, French Croix de Guerre, one of Britain's greatest aces, who managed to escape von Richthofen's attentions back on 27 December 1916. (see page 95)

McCudden was born on 28 March 1895, one of four sons of a corporal in the Royal Engineers, of whom three were to be killed while flying. Educated in army schools, he joined the Royal Engineers as a boy soldier on 26 April 1910 and was regraded as a bugler six months later. In 1913 he was accepted into the RFC as a second class air mechanic. Despite having no formal engineering training, his enthusiasm and curiosity in all mechanical things gave him a sound knowledge of engines. In June 1913 he was posted to No. 3 Squadron where he never lost an opportunity to fly as a passenger. He moved to France with 3 Squadron on 13 August 1914 and in May 1915 recognition of his abilities was rewarded with promotion to sergeant in charge of all engine maintenance in the unit. Continuing to fly as much as possible, including some unofficial pilot instruction, he re-mustered as an observer. After a number of engagements with the enemy, McCudden received the French *Croix de Guerre*.

In January 1916 McCudden got his wish and returned to the UK for pilot training. After tuition at Gosport, he obtained his Royal Aero Club 'ticket', No. 2745, on 16 April 1916. On completion of his

McCudden's grave at Wavans in 1918 with the original wooden cross.

training he was posted to 20 Squadron, who were flying the ungainly, but effective, FE2 from Clairmarais, near St Omer. He was only with them a month before he achieved his ambition and was transferred to 29 Squadron, a fighter unit, a few miles to the east. They were flying the DH2 and on 6 September 1916 he scored his first victory. At the time of his action with von Richthofen he had claimed one victory. He had a number of indecisive engagements and received the Military Medal before being promoted from sergeant to second lieutenant. By February 1917 he had claimed five victories and received the MC, but on the 23rd was posted home.

After a number of training appointments, where one of his pupils was his younger brother he returned to France in command of B Flight of 56 Squadron. This was Ball's old squadron but McCudden's attitude to air fighting was completely different. Where Ball would attack anything, regardless of odds, McCudden's keen and analytical mind viewed each situation from a tactical point. Never afraid to attack he would, nevertheless, withdraw from a fight if it was disadvantageous. He was determined that his flight would be the best and he imposed meticulous maintenance standards on his ground crews and pressed the need for teamwork. On 18 August 1917 McCudden claimed his first victory with 56 Squadron, sending an Albatros scout spinning down out of control. In the next two days he claimed three more.

On 23 September 1917 McCudden's flight, together with C Flight, were involved in one of the best known aerial battles of the First World War, when the great ace Werner Voss was shot down and killed (see page 18). McCudden spent a lot of time refining his aeroplane and honing his skills. In December he was awarded the DSO. During December 56 Squadron had claimed eighteen German machines, of which McCudden's share was fourteen! In January a bar to his DSO was promulgated. On 1 March 1918 McCudden flew his last sortie in 56 Squadron. In just five months he had claimed 52 enemy aircraft, 40% of the squadron total.

On 9 July 1918 some eighteen months after the encounter with von Richthofen, McCudden was flying out from England to take command of 60 Squadron based at Boffles. The site of the airfield is to the north-east of Auxi-le-Chateau, right off the D941, mid-way between Auxi and Frévent.

McCudden lost his bearings and so landed at Auxi to ask for directions. Taking off again to fly the short distance to Boffles, his engine suddenly cut out and he was tragically killed in the resulting crash.

Robert Alexander Little

Little, an Australian from Melbourne, was born in July 1895. Flying Pups, Triplanes and Camels with 8 Naval Squadron and 203 Squadron RAF, he had scored 47 victories by May 1918 and won the DSO & Bar, and the DSC & Bar, plus the French *Croix de Guerre*, but had been mortally wounded attacking a Gotha bomber at night on 27 May. He crashed and bled to death before anyone could find the crash site.

Continue ahead on the D938 and then the D941 into Auxi-le-Château. Turn right on the D119 to Hesdin and Berck. Follow the D928 towards Hesdin then turn left on the D119 to Berck. At the N1 turn right for the A16. At a roundabout go left on the D303 to Boulogne. At another roundabout go left on the A16 to Boulogne. Exit the A16 at junction 26 and at the roundabout turn right for Étaples. At the next roundabout go ahead on the D940 to Boulogne. Continue ahead on the D940 and after leaving Étaples the cemetery will appear on the left.

Robert Little DSO DSC has his grave two rows behind that of McCudden.

Étaples Military Cemetery and Centre

There could hardly be a greater contrast between Wavans, one of the smallest and most intimate of Western Front cemeteries, and Étaples. The largest British military cemetery in France, and the second largest on the Western Front after Tyne Cot, to the east of Ypres. It contains 10,769 First World War Commonwealth burials as well as over 650 German ones.

The cemetery, designed by Sir Edwin Lutyens, is most impressive, being approached down a hill from the road, and the entrance is surmounted by large carved stone flags.

With excellent port facilities and rail links to the Front, the whole area was a vast training, supply, and hospital area throughout the First World War. Remote from anything except air attack, at any time up to 100,000 troops could be camped in the general area.

One area of the training grounds was known as 'The Bullring', the scene of supposed mutiny towards the end of the war, in practice little more than disturbances about conditions in the rear areas. These were the background for the controversial television programme *The Monocled Mutineer*, although as the central character, Percy Topliss was aboard a troop ship on his way to South Africa at the time, the story might be taken with a pinch of salt!

The medical facilities, which included eleven general, one stationary, four Red Cross hospitals and a convalescent depot, could house some 22,000 wounded and sick, and even in September 1919, ten months after the war, three hospitals and the QMAAC convalescent depot remained.

Despite all the medical facilities here, many of the wounded still succumbed to their injuries, hence the enormous number of casualties interred here.

There are 45 members of the air service in the cemetery, one of whom is a victim of von Richthofen. He is Frederick Andrews, whose grave is in plot XVII, which is the first plot as you walk down the steps from the entrance and is just left of centre in the front row.

Frederick Seymour Andrews (XVII A 11)

Second Lieutenant Andrews was a 'Bloody April' casualty, the observer to Lieutenant A Pascoe of 13 Squadron. They were shot down on the afternoon of 16 April 1917, von Richthofen's forty-fifth victory.

They had taken off at 1450 hours on artillery observation duties over the British XVII Corp's front. They were attacked by von Richthofen at about 2,500 feet. He managed to approach unnoticed, and opened fire, the plane going down between Bailleul and Gavrelle on the British side of the lines. Pascoe got their BE2e down in a forced landing but a strong wind blew the machine over and it was later heavily shelled by the Germans.

Frederick Andrews was born in 1889, the son of Thomas Frederick and Louisa G Andrews of Warden Street, Harrismith, Orange Free State, South Africa. He was educated at Mercheston College and School in Harrismith.

He travelled to England to volunteer for the forces, and to visit his uncle, also Frederick Andrews, at his home in Handsworth Wood Road, Handsworth, Birmingham. His uncle ran an engineering company, F Andrews & Company, Brunswick Works, Cheston Street, Aston, Birmingham.

Young Frederick joined the Royal Flying Corps and initially served in the ranks with 1 Squadron, reporting for duty with them in France on 15 August 1916. He was later selected for a commission, and gazetted second lieutenant on the General List in March 1917, then posted to 53 Squadron, where he joined up with his pilot, Alphonso Pascoe. The two were posted as a crew to 13 Squadron on 18 March 1917, just four weeks before they were shot down.

Removed from the wreckage of the BE2e, Andrews was passed through a succession of medical facilities, finally reaching Le Touquet Hospital where he died of his injuries thirteen days later.

Alphonso Pascoe was the son of Edward and Jane Pascoe of 'Fernleigh', Godolphin Road, Helston, Cornwall. He obtained his Royal Aero Club Aviators Certificate, No. 3664, on 28 September 1916. After further training, he was awarded his wings, and was posted to 53 Squadron in January 1917 where he met up with his observer, Frederick Andrews. Pascoe was also injured, returning to England to recover from his wounds.

Lieutenant A Pascoe, 13 Squadron, wounded 16 April 1917. His observer, Second Lieutenant F S Andrews, died at Le Touquet and is buried in Étaples cemetery. They were the Baron's 45th victory.

Continue ahead on the D940 and rejoin the A16 and proceed north to Calais. This concludes *In the Footsteps of the Red Baron*.

Conclusion

For those readers whose interest in First World War aviation may have been aroused by this present book I can recommend joining *Cross and Cockade International – The First World War Aviation Historical Society*. The membership secretary's address is:

Membership Secretary
Cross and Cockade International
11 Francis Drive
Westward Ho!
EX39 1XE
e-mail: cci@blueyonder.co.uk
website: http://www.crossandcockade.com

I can also recommend *Over the Front,* the journal of The League of World War I Aviation Historians. Their membership secretary's address is:

Membership Secretary
The League of World War I Aviation Historians
16820 25th Ave. N.
Plymouth
MN 55447-2228
USA
e-mail: dpolglaze@comcast.net
website: http://www.overthefront.com

In addition, the authors are interested in contacting First World War aviators or their relatives, whether they figure in this book or not.

Mike O'Connor's e-mail address is:
oconnor@stonehousecottage.freeserve.co.uk

Norman Franks' e-mail address is:
x4hej@yahoo.co.uk

Further Reading

A Selected Bibliography

Under the Guns of the Red Baron, Franks, Giblin and McCrery, Grub Street 2000.

The Red Baron's Last Flight, N Franks and A Bennett, Grub Street 1997.

The Red Air Fighter, M von Richthofen, The Aeroplane and General Publishing Co 1918.

Who Killed the Red Baron?, P J Carisella and J W Ryan, White Lion Publishers 1969.

The Day the Red Baron Died, D M Titler, Ian Allan 1973.

Richthofen, Beyond the Legend of the Red Baron, P Kilduff, Arms and Armour Press 1993.

The Red Baron Combat Wing, P Kilduff, Arms and Armour Press1997.

Mother of Eagles, S H Fischer, Schiffer Publishing Ltd 2001.

Hunting with Richthofen, J Hayzlett, Grub Street 1996.

The Red Knight of Germany, Floyd Gibbons, Cassell 1930.

Von Richthofen and the Flying Circus, H J Nowarra and K S Brown, Harleyford Publications Ltd 1959.

Courage Remembered, Kingsley Ward and E Gibson, HMSO 1989.

The Sky Their Battlefield, Trevor Henshaw, Grub Street 1995.

Airmen Died in the Great War, Chris Hobson, Hayward and Son 1995.

Aviation Awards of Imperial Germany in World War I Vols 1-6, Neal W O'Connor, Foundation for World War I Aviation , 1988-1999.

Under the Guns of the German Aces, N Franks and H Giblin, Grub Street 1997.

Albert Ball VC, Chaz Bowyer, William Kimber and Co 1977.

Sagittarius Rising, Cecil Lewis, Peter Davies 1936.

For Valour The Air VCs, Chaz Bowyer,William Kimber and Co 1978.

High in the Empty Blue, The History of 56 Squadron RFC/RAF 1916-1919, Alex Revell, Flying Machines Press 1995.

Flying Corps Headquarters 1914-18, Maurice Baring, William Heinemann 1930.

Flying Fury, J T B McCudden, Jonathan Hamilton Ltd., 1930.

Airco DH2, Windsock Datafile No. 48, B J Gray, Albatros Publications 1994.

Hawker VC, Tyrrel M Hawker, Mitre Press 1965.

A History of 24 Squadron Royal Air Force, A E Illingworth, The Aeroplane and General Publishing Co 1920.

Ace of the Iron Cross, Ernst Udet, Newnes 1937.

Pictorial History of the German Army Air Service, Alex Imrie, Ian Allan 1971.

The Royal Flying Corps in France, Ralph Barker (Two volumes), Constable 1994 and 1995.

The Jasta Pilots, Franks/Bailey/Duiven, Grub Street 1996.

Above the Trenches, Shores, Franks and Guest, Grub Street 1990.

Above the Lines, Franks, Bailey and Guest, Grub Street 1993.

The Jasta War Chronology, Franks, Bailey and Duiven, Grub Street 1998.

Bloody April, Alan Morris, Jarrolds 1967.

Bloody April, Black September, Franks, Guest and Bailey, Grub Street, 1995.

The Fokker Triplane, Alex Imrie, Arms and Armour 1992.

The Aeroplanes of the Royal Flying Corps (Military Wing), J M Bruce, Putnams 1982.

APPENDICES

Appendix A

Names of Von Richthofen's Victims
on the Arras Memorial

Name	Rank	Sqdn	Date of death	Vic
Applin, R	Lieutenant	19 Sqn	29 Apr 1917	49
Baldwin, C G	Sergeant	18 Sqn	3 Nov 1916	7
Barford, K P	Lieutenant	2 Sqn	27 Mar 1918	72
Barlow, H C	Lieutenant	9 Sqn	18 Jun 1917	53
Beebee, A	Acting Corporal	18 Sqn	29 Apr 1917	50
Bellerby, H	Sergeant	27 Sqn	23 Sept 1916	2
Bentham, G A	2nd Lieutenant	18 Sqn	3 Nov 1916	7
Betley, E	2nd Lieutenant	82 Sqn	28 Mar 1918	74
Bonner, P	1st Air Mechanic	13 Sqn	2 Apr 1917	32
Bowman, L S	Lieutenant	53 Sqn	25 Jun 1917	56
Cameron, D	2nd Lieutenant	3 Sqn	25 Mar 1918	68
Cantle, L H	Lieutenant	43 Sqn	8 Apr 1917	38
Cuzner, A E	Flight Sub Lt	8 (N) Sqn	29 Apr 1917	52
D'Arcy, L G	Lieutenant	18 Sqn	20 Dec 1916	14
Davies, D E	Lieutenant	12 Sqn	29 Apr 1917	51
Denovan, A M	2nd Lieutenant	1 Sqn	26 Mar 1918	69
Ellis, R W E	Lieutenant	9 Sqn	18 Jun 1917	53
Fenwick, W C	2nd Lieutenant	21 Sqn	7 Oct 1916	4
Follit, R W	Lieutenant	13 Sqn	28 Apr 1917	48
Hawker, L G (VC)	Major	24 Sqn	23 Nov 1916	11
Jones, E D	Lieutenant	52 Sqn	2 Apr 1918	75
Leggat, M	2nd Lieutenant	15 Sqn	26 Mar 1918	70
MacGregor, D A D I	Lieutenant	41 Sqn	30 Nov 1917	63
McCone, J P	Lieutenant	41 Sqn	24 Mar 1918	67

Name	Rank	Sqdn	Date of death	Vic
McNaughton, N G	Captain	57 Sqn	24 Jun 1917	55
Mearns, A H	Lieutenant	57 Sqn	24 Jun 1917	55
Newton, R F	2nd Lieutenant	52 Sqn	2 Apr 1918	75
O'Bierne, J I M	2nd Lieutenant	25 Sqn	3 Apr 1917	34
Pascoe, F G B	2nd Lieutenant	53 Sqn	2 Jul 1917	57
Pearson, A J	Lieutenant	29 Sqn	9 Mar 1917	25
Powell, P J G	Lieutenant	13 Sqn	2 Apr 1917	32
Rathbone, G H	Lieutenant	12 Sqn	29 Apr 1917	51
Raymond-Barker, R	Major	3 Sqn	20 Apr 1918	79
Reading, V J	2nd Lieutenant	15 Sqn	26 Mar 1918	70
Smart, E T	Lieutenant	2 Sqn	27 Mar 1918	72
Smart, G O	2nd Lieutenant	60 Sqn	7 Apr 1917	37
Smith, S P	Captain	46 Sqn	6 Apr 1918	76
Stead, G	Sergeant	18 Sqn	29 Apr 1917	50
Stuart, J M	Captain	59 Sqn	13 Apr 1917	41
Taylor, J B	2nd Lieutenant	82 Sqn	28 Mar 1918	74
Todd, A S	Flight Lieutenant	8 (N) Sqn	4 Jan 1917	16
Whatley, H A	Sergeant	53 Sqn	2 Jul 1917	57
Whiteside, R C	Sub Lieutenant	18 Sqn	20 Dec 1916	14
Williams, C P	2nd Lieutenant	19 Sqn	26 Aug 1917	59
Wood, M H	Lieutenant	59 Sqn	13 Apr 1917	41

Appendix B

Casualties in Cemeteries involved with the Red Baron as they appear in the Tours

Harlebeke	W H T Williams – victory No. 58; W Kember – victory No. 60
Strand	J E Power Clutterbuck – victory No. 56
Bailleul	D C Cunnell
Aire	J Hay – victory No. 17
Bruay	G M Watt and E A Howlett – victory No. 28; S H Quicke – victory No. 29
Barlin	G M Gosset-Bibby and G J O Britchta – victory No. 24
Aubigny	W J Lidsey – victory No. 29
Bois Carré	P W Murray and D J McRae – victory No. 19 K I MacKenzie and G Everingham – victory No. 39
Petit Vimy	E A Welch and A G Tollervey – victory No. 47
Canadian No. 2 Neuville-St-Vaast	A E Boultbee and F King – victory No. 27
Cabaret Rouge	H A Croft – victory No. 20; R Dunn – victory No. 33 H J Green and A W Reid – victory No. 23 J Smyth and E G Byrne – victory No. 26
Vermelles	G W B Hampton – victory No. 21

Noyelles-Godault	A H Bates and W A Barnes – victory No. 43
Douai	H D K George – victory No. 35
Auberchicourt	R W Farquhar – victory No. 54
Porte-de-Paris	L B F Morris – victory No. 1
	G S Hall – victory No. 10
Villers-Plouich	T Rees – victory No. 1
Lebucquière	J Thompson – victory No. 5
Bancourt	E C Lansdale and A Clarkson – victory No. 3
	A J Fisher – victory No. 6
Achiet-le-Grand	J G Cameron – victory No. 8
	G Doughty – victory No. 10
Douchy-les-Ayette	A G Knight – victory No. 13
Dive Copse	G H Harding – victory No. 73
Wavans	J T B McCudden VC – victory No. 15
Étaples	F S Andrews – victory No. 45

Appendix C

Airfields from where von Richthofen operated
when claiming his victories

Victory	Date	Crew	Sqn	Cemetery/Fate
Bertincourt	*27 Aug-24 Sept 1916*			
1 FE2b	17 Sept 1916	L B F Morris	11	Porte-de-Paris
		T Rees		Plouich
2 G100	23 Sept 1916	H Bellerby	27	Arras Memorial
Lagnicourt	*24 Sept-5 Dec 1916*			
3 FE2b	30 Sept 1916	E C Lansdale	11	Bancourt
		A Clarkson		Bancourt
4 BE12	7 Oct 1916	W C Fenwick	21	Arras Memorial
5 BE12	16 Oct 1916	J Thompson	19	Lebucquière
6 BE12	25 Oct 1916	A J Fisher	21	Bancourt
7 FE2b	3 Nov 1916	C G Baldwin	18	Arras Memorial
		G A Bentham		Arras Memorial
8 BE2c	9 Nov 1916	J G Cameron	12	Achiet-le-Grand
9 BE2c	20 Nov 1916	T H Clarke	15	PoW
		J C Lees		PoW
10 FE2b	20 Nov 1916	G S Hall	18	Porte-de-Paris
		G Doughty		Achiet-le-Grand
11 DH2	23 Nov 1916	L G Hawker	24	Arras Memorial
Pronville	*5 Dec 1916-14 Jan 1917*			
12 DH2	11 Dec 1916	B P G Hunt	32	PoW
13 DH2	20 Dec 1916	A G Knight	29	Douchy-les-Ayette

Victory	Date	Crew	Sqn	Cemetery/Fate
14 FE2b	20 Dec 1916	L G D'Arcy	18	Arras Memorial
		R C Whiteside		Arras Memorial
15 DH2	27 Dec 1916	J T B McCudden	29	Safe (KIFA1918)
16 Pup	4 Jan 1917	A S Todd	8N	Arras Memorial

La Brayelle *15 Jan 1917-14 Apr 1917*

17 FE8	23 Jan 1917	J Hay	40	Aire
18 FE2b	24 Jan 1917	O Greig	25	PoW
		J E MacLennan		PoW
19 BE2d	1 Feb 1917	P W Murray	16	Bois-Carré
		D J McRae		Bois-Carré
20 BE2d	14 Feb 1917	C D Bennett	2	PoW
		H A Croft		Cabaret Rouge
21 BE2c	14 Feb 1917	G C Bailey	2	WIA/Safe
		G W B Hampton		Safe (KIA 1917)
22 BE2d	4 March 1917	J B E Crosbee	2	Safe
		J E Prance	16	WIA (Died1918)
23 Sop 1½	4 Mar 1917	H J Green	43	Cabaret Rouge
		A W Reid		Cabaret Rouge
24 BE2e	6 Mar 1917	G M Gosset-Bibby	16	Barlin
		G J O Brichta		Barlin
25 DH2	9 Mar 1917	A J Pearson	29	Arras Memorial
26 BE2d	11 Mar 1917	J Smyth	2	Cabaret Rouge
		E G Byrne		Cabaret Rouge
27 FE2b	17 Mar 1917	A E Boultbee	25	Canadian No.2
		F King		Canadian No.2
28 BE2g	17 Mar 1917	G MacD Watt	16	Bruay
		E A Howlett		Bruay

Victory	Date	Crew	Sqn	Cemetery/Fate
29 BE2f	21 Mar 1917	S H Quicke	16	Bruay
		W J Lidsey		Aubigny
30 Spad 7	24 Mar 1917	R P Baker	19	WIA/PoW
31 Nieup 17	25 Mar 1917	C G Gilbert	29	PoW
32 BE2d	2 Apr 1917	P J G Powell	13	Arras Memorial
		P Bonner		Arras Memorial
33 Sop 1½	2 Apr 1917	A P Warren	43	PoW
		R Dunn		Cabaret Rouge
34 FE2d	3 Apr 1917	D P McDonald	25	PoW
		J I M O'Beirne		Arras Memorial
35 BF2a	5 Apr 1917	A N Lechler	48	WIA/PoW
		H D K George		Douai
36 BF2a	5 Apr 1917	A T Adams	48	PoW
		D J Stewart		PoW
37 Nieup 17	7 Apr 1917	G O Smart	60	Arras Memorial
38 Sop 1½	8 Apr 1917	J S Heagerty	43	WIA/PoW
		L H Cantle		Arras Memorial
39 BE2g	8 Apr 1917	K I MacKenzie	16	Bois-Carré
		G Everingham		Bois-Carré
40 BE2c	11 Apr 1917	E C E Derwin	13	Safe (KIFA1918)
		H Pierson		Safe/WIA
41 RE8	13 Apr 1917	J M Stuart	59	Arras Memorial
		M H Wood		Arras Memorial
42 FE2b	13 Apr 1917	J A Cunniffe	11	Safe
		W J Batten		Safe
43 FE2b	13 Apr 1917	A H Bates	25	Noyelles-Godault
		W A Barnes		Noyelles-Godault
44 Nieup 17	14 Apr 1917	W O Russell	60	PoW

Victory	Date	Crew	Sqn	Cemetery/Fate
Roucourt	*15 Apr-9 Jun 1917*			
45 BE2e	16 Apr 1917	A Pascoe	13	WIA but safe
		F S Andrews		Étaples
46 FE2b	22 Apr 1917	W Franklin	11	WIA
		W F Fletcher		Injured
47 BE2f	23 Apr 1917	E A Welch	16	Petit Vimy
		A G Tollervey		Petit Vimy
48 BE2e	28 Apr 1917	R W Follit	13	Arras Memorial
		F J Kirkham		WIA/PoW
49 Spad 7	29 Apr 1917	R Applin	19	Arras Memorial
50 FE2d	29 Apr 1917	G Stead	18	Arras Memorial
		A Beebee		Arras Memorial
51 BE2e	29 Apr 1917	D E Davies	12	Arras Memorial
		G H Rathbone		Arras Memorial
52 Triplane	29 Apr 1917	A E Cuzner	8N	Arras Memorial
Harlebeke	*10 Jun-1 Jul 1917*			
53 RE8	18 Jun 1917	R W E Ellis	9	Arras Memorial
		H C Barlow		Arras Memorial
54 Spad 7	23 Jun 1917	R W Farquhar	23	Safe
55 DH4	24 Jun 1917	N G McNaughton	57	Arras Memorial
		A H Mearns		Arras Memorial
56 RE8	25 Jun 1917	L S Bowman	53	Arras Memorial
		J E Power Clutterbuck		Strand
Marckebeke	*2 Jul-22 Nov 1917*			
57 RE8	2 Jul 1917	H A Whatley	53	Arras Memorial

Victory	Date	Crew	Sqn	Cemetery/Fate
		F G B Pascoe		Arras Memorial
58 Nieup 23	16 Aug 1917	W H T Williams	29	Harlebeke
59 Spad 7	26 Aug 1917	C P Williams	19	Arras Memorial
60 RE8	1 Sep 1917	J B C Madge	6	WIA/PoW
		W Kember		Harlebeke
61 Pup	3 Sep 1917	A F Bird	46	PoW

Avesnes-le-Sec *22 Nov 1917-20 Mar 1918*

Victory	Date	Crew	Sqn	Cemetery/Fate
62 DH5	23 Nov 1917	J A V Boddy	64	WIA/Safe
63 SE5a	30 Nov 1917	D A D I MacGregor	41	Arras Memorial
64 BF2b	12 Mar 1918	L C F Clutterbuck	62	PoW
		H J Sparks		WIA/PoW
65 Camel	13 Mar 1918	E E Heath	73	WIA/PoW
66 Camel	18 Mar 1918	W G Ivamy	54	PoW

Awoingt *21 Mar-25 Mar 1918*

Victory	Date	Crew	Sqn	Cemetery/Fate
67 SE5a	24 Mar 1918	J P McCone	41	Arras Memorial
68 Camel	25 Mar 1918	D Cameron	3	Arras Memorial

Léchelle *26 Mar-11 Apr 1918*

Victory	Date	Crew	Sqn	Cemetery/Fate
69 SE5a	26 Mar 1918	A McN Denovan	1	Arras Memorial
70 RE8	26 Mar 1918	V J Reading	15	Arras Memorial
		M Leggat		Arras Memorial
71 Camel	27 Mar 1918	T S Sharpe	73	WIA/PoW
72 AWFK8	27 Mar 1918	E T Smart	2	Arras Memorial
		K P Barford		Arras Memorial
73 Dolphin	27 Mar 1918	G H Harding	79	Dive Copse

Victory	Date	Crew	Sqn	Cemetery/Fate
74 AWFK8	28 Mar 1918	J B Taylor	82	Arras Memorial
		E Betley		Arras Memorial
75 RE8	2 Apr 1918	E D Jones	52	Arras Memorial
		R F Newton		Arras Memorial
76 Camel	6 Apr 1918	S P Smith	46	Arras Memorial
77 Camel	7 Apr 1918	A V Gallie	73	Safe
78 Camel	7 Apr 1918	R G H Adams	73	WIA/PoW

Cappy *12 Apr 1918-*

Victory	Date	Crew	Sqn	Cemetery/Fate
79 Camel	20 Apr 1918	R Raymond-Barker	3	Arras Memorial
80 Camel	20 Apr 1918	D G Lewis	3	PoW

Index

174

175

Minifie, R, 85
Morlancourt Ridge, 121, 133-134, 135, 138, 139, 140, 143
Morris, Second Lieutenant L B F, 91, 100-101, 103, 108-109
Mottershead, T, 35
Müller, *Vizefeldwebel* H K, 113
Murray, Lieutenant P W, 48

Pascoe, Lieutenant A, 156, 157
Pascoe, F G B, 26
Paustian, S, 123
Plum Farm, Frezenberg, 20
Popkin, Sergeant C, 140, 141-142
Powell, P J B, 61
Power Clutterbuck, Second Lieutenant J E, 15, 24, 32, 33-34
Proville, 93

Quicke, Flight Sergeant S H, 39, 40, 45

Ray, Franz, 100
Raymond-Barker, A, 86, 87
Raymond-Barker, Major R, 86-87, 130
Rees, J, 103
Rees, Major L W B, 63
Rees, Lieutenant (later Captain) T, 91, 101, 103-104, 109
Reid, Second Lieutenant A W, 60-61
Reinhard, *Oberleutnant* W, 129
Rhys Davids, Lieutenant A P F, 20
Richardson, L L, 48
Richthofen, Major A von, 122
Richthofen, *Oberleutnant* L von, 51, 61, 74, 81, 122
Richthofen, *Rittmeister* M von, 11-12
  illustrations, 5, 7, 19, 28, 69, 77, 81, 93, 122, 136
  wounded, 30, 31-33
  death, 137-142, 146
Robinson, Captain W L, 71
Roucourt, Château de, 74, 75, 76-78
Rowley, V, 85

Ste Colette Brickworks, 121, 133, 134-135, 138, 139, 143
Schäfer, K, 64
Schröder, *Leutnant* H, 32, 33
Seymour, F S, 121
Sharpe, Captain T S, 126, 127
Simpson, J C, 63
Smart, Second Lieutenant G O, 88-89
Smith, Captain S P, 126, 128-129
Smyth, Second Lieutenant J, 58-59
Steinhauser, *Leutnant*, 81

Taylor, Second Lieutenant J B, 107
Thompson, Second Lieutenant J, 109-110
Thomsen, General H von der, 5
Todd, Flight Lieutenant A S, 88
Tollervey, Sergeant A G, 47, 51, 52
Trenchard, General H, 85

Vaux-sur-Somme, 121, 134, 138
Villers-Bretonneux Australian Memorial, 121, 142-143
Vimy Ridge, 53
Voss, W, 15, 18-20, 28, 61, 154

Walz, F, 56
Warren, Second Lieutenant A P, 61-63
Watt, G M, 39-40, 54
Weiss, *Leutnant* H, 129, 136, 137
Welch, Second Lieutenant E A, 47, 51-52
Wells, Second Lieutenant H M W, 53
Wervicq-Sud, 15, 31-33, 36
Whatley, H A, 26
Williams, C P, 26
Williams, Lieutenant W H T, 15, 21-22, 26
Wolff, K, 28, 29, 76, 77, 110
Woodbridge, Lieutenant A E, 31, 36
Wüsthoff, *Leutnant* K, 129

Zeumer, G, 17